The Cassel Commentary

Philippians

Dr. Doug Cassel

The Cassel Commentary

Philippians

Dr. Doug Cassel

The Cassel Commentary, Philippians

All Scripture quotations are taken from the King James Authorized Bible

ISBN-13: 978-0692503560

Printed in the United States of America

Table of Contents

Introduction

Dr. Cassel has written the consummate commentary on Philippians. As you read his insights into this epistle, you will find a wonderful mixture of history, geography, biography and theology, each baptized with knowledgeable insight into the culture and customs of the time period. Yet there is another element present that is too often missing in similar works — a heart-felt love for the scriptures themselves. Dr. Cassel's view of Philippians is shaped by his pastoral experience, his soul winning zeal, and his passion for world-wide missions. With great respect for the Word of God, he has delivered a commentary that will be valuable to the newest convert as well as to the seasoned saint.

Prepare to be blessed!

Pastor Jerry Ross, Jasonville, Indiana

Introduction To Philippians

Acts 16:1-40 *Then came he to Derbe and Lystra: and, behold, a certain disciple was there, named Timotheus, the son of a certain woman, which was a Jewess, and believed; but his father was a Greek: Which was well reported of by the brethren that were at Lystra and Iconium. Him would Paul have to go forth with him; and took and circumcised him because of the Jews which were in those quarters: for they knew all that his father was a Greek. And as they went through the cities, they delivered them the decrees for to keep, that were ordained of the apostles and elders which were at Jerusalem. And so were the churches established in the faith, and increased in number daily. Now when they had gone throughout Phrygia and the region of Galatia, and were forbidden of the Holy Ghost to preach the word in Asia, After they were come to Mysia, they assayed to go into Bithynia: but the Spirit suffered them not. And they passing by Mysia came down to Troas. And a vision appeared to Paul in the night; There stood a man of Macedonia, and prayed him, saying, Come over into Macedonia, and help us. And after he had seen the vision, immediately we endeavoured to go into Macedonia, assuredly gathering that the Lord had called us for to preach the gospel unto them. Therefore loosing from Troas, we came with a straight course to Samothracia, and the next day to Neapolis; And from thence to Philippi, which is the chief city of that part of Macedonia, and a colony: and we were in that city abiding certain days. And on the sabbath we went out of the city by a river side, where prayer* was wont to be made; and we sat down, and spake unto the women which resorted thither. And a certain woman named Lydia, a seller of purple, of the city of Thyatira, which worshipped God, heard us: whose heart the Lord opened, that she attended unto the things which were spoken of Paul. And when she was baptized, and her household, she besought us, saying, If ye have judged me to be faithful to the Lord, come into my house, and abide there. And she constrained us. And it came to pass, as we went to prayer, a certain damsel possessed with a spirit of divination met us, which brought her masters much gain by soothsaying: The same followed Paul and us, and cried, saying, These men are the servants of the most high God, which shew unto us the way of salvation. And this did she many days. But Paul, being grieved, turned and said to the spirit, I command thee in the name of Jesus Christ to come out of her. And he came out the same hour. And when her masters saw that the hope of their gains was gone, they caught Paul and Silas, and drew them into the marketplace unto the rulers, And brought them to the magistrates, saying, These men, being Jews, do exceedingly trouble our city, And teach customs, which are not lawful for us to receive, neither to observe, being Romans. And the multitude rose up together against them: and the magistrates rent off their clothes, and commanded to beat them. And when they had laid many stripes upon them, they cast them into prison, charging the jailor to keep them safely: Who, having received such a charge, thrust them into the inner prison, and made their feet fast in the stocks. And at midnight Paul and Silas prayed, and sang praises unto God: and the prisoners *heard them. And suddenly there was a great earthquake, so that the foundations of the prison were shaken: and immediately all the doors were opened, and every one's bands were loosed. And the keeper of the prison awaking out of his sleep, and seeing the prison doors open, he drew out his sword, and would have killed himself, supposing that the prisoners had been fled. But Paul cried with a loud voice, saying, Do thyself no harm: for we are all here. Then he called for a light, and sprang in, and came trembling, and fell down before Paul and Silas, And brought them out, and said, Sirs, what must I do to be saved? And they said, Believe on the Lord Jesus Christ, and thou shalt be saved, and thy house. And they spake unto him the word of the Lord, and to all that were in his house. And he took them the same hour of the night, and washed their stripes; and was baptized, he and all his, straightway. And when he had brought them into his house, he set meat before them, and rejoiced, believing in God with all his house. And when it was day, the magistrates sent the serjeants, saying, Let those men go. And the keeper of the prison told this saying to Paul, The magistrates have sent to let you go: now therefore depart, and go in peace. But Paul said unto them, They have beaten us openly uncondemned, being Romans, and have cast us into prison; and now do they thrust us out privily? nay verily; but let them come themselves and fetch us out. And the serjeants told these words unto the magistrates: and they feared, when they heard that they were Romans. And they came and besought them, and brought them out, and desired them to depart out of the city. And they went out of the prison, and entered into the house of Lydia: and when they had seen the brethren, they comforted them, and departed.*

The City

Philippi lies at the southwest corner of Europe in Macedonia. Macedonia is the northern part of present day Greece. Philippi was first named Krenides which means *"The wells"* or *"fountains"*, according to Strabo, the ancient Greek geographer, philosopher and historian. It was noted for its gold and silver mines. The gold and silver mines date back to the ancient Phoenician empire but were all played out by the time of Christianity. It derives its name from Philip II, the father of Alexander the Great. Philip II was the king of Macedonia. He took this city from the Thracians in 358-357 BC and gave it his name. Philippi means *"fond of horses."* Philippi was a strategic city on the Great Northern Highway between the east and the west. There was a range of hills, the Pangaion mountains, that divided Asia and Europe from east to west. At Philippi the range of hills dip into a pass. To cross through the pass from Asia into Europe and vice-a-versa one must travel through Philippi.

Great battles were fought on the plains of Philippi. Julius Caesar fought Pompey the Great. It was on the plains of Philippi in 42 BC that the famous Battle of Philippi was fought. Octavius and Antony defeated Cassius and Brutus avenging the assassination of Julius Caesar two years prior in 44 BC. Octavius and Anthony confiscated Cicero's property, along with other wealthy Romans, and sold it in order to raise an army to march on Cicero's friends-Brutus and Cassius. This was the final battle in the Wars of the Second Triumvirate (Octavius and Antony) against the forces of the tyrannicides (Brutus and Cassius). Antony had to leave a sick Octavius behind in Epidamnus so the glory of the battle went to Antony. Both Brutus and Cassius committed suicide. The Roman Republic fell and the Roman Empire was born. The Philippi that Paul knew was made a Roman military colony by Antony after his victory over Brutus and Cassius.

The city of Philippi was a Roman colony. The term "colony" carried a different meaning in Paul's day than it does in our lifetime today. A Roman colony was a foreign city that had demonstrated loyalty by some admirable act of devotion. Rome would reward that city by conferring on them the title of "Colonia." That meant that everyone who was born free in that city was granted Roman citizenship. They had the same rights and privileges as any citizen of Rome. Years before Paul wrote Philippians, Rome was at war with the people of the northeast in Macedonia. When the Roman army reached the Macedonian city of Philippi, they found a Philippian army ready to join them and a wealth of material resources made available to them. The Roman general was so pleased by their generosity and loyalty that he sent back to Rome a report and a request on behalf of the city. The Roman Senate met and conferred upon Philippi the title of "Colonia." Every man in Philippi could now say that he was a Roman citizen.

Rome also used colonies as a great method for expanding and keeping her empire intact. Many soldiers of Rome were slaves. After a period of faithful military service, they would be granted citizenship. Many men enlisted into the Roman army. They would obtain wages and eventually citizenship instead of simple slavery for daily bread and shelter, which was often poor and little. Whenever the term of enlistment was up for these veterans, Rome would send them out in groups of three hundred with their wives and children. Rome would make them a colony in some key geographical location. Theses colonies became the dots that connected the roads that all led to Rome. These strategic outposts were maintained by veterans who would make up an able-bodied militia at any moment. They could be sent from one colony to another in a moment of crises. As a result, these colonies became little fragments of Rome. These colonies were very proud of their Roman citizenship. They spoke the Roman language, wore Roman clothes, observed the customs of Rome and the magistrates held Roman titles. You can hear the sound of Roman pride as the Philippians accused Paul and Silas: *Acts 16:20-21 And brought them to the magistrates, saying, These men, being Jews, do exceedingly trouble our city, And teach customs, which are not lawful for us to receive, neither to observe, being Romans.* Just as the Roman colonists never forgot that they were Romans simply because they lived in Philippi, so too the Philippian believers were never to forget they were Christians and citizens of Heaven, though they also lived in Philippi. There was also a school of medicine in Philippi. There are many that believe that Luke was from Philippi. Indeed, he did remain there for a time after Paul left. Luke caught up with Paul later down the missionary trail.

The Church

Philippi was the first church Paul planted in Europe. He first came to Philippi while on his second missionary journey. His companions were Luke, Silas and Timothy. Philippi was a Roman military colony in Macedonia (present day Greece) and probably had very few Jews living there.

Paul and Barnabas had separated after their first missionary journey. Paul attempted to go south into Asia where Ephesus was a large and leading city. The Holy Spirit forbid them from going-Acts 16:6. Paul then thought he would go north into present day Turkey. But when...*they assayed to go into Bithynia...the Spirit suffered them not-Acts 16:7.* Paul's plans were not God's plans. Paul could not go north or south. He had come from the east and so he went as far west as Troas. To go west of Troas required sailing across the Aegean Sea. While in Troas, Paul had a vision of a man crying for him to come over to Macedonia and help them. We even sing of the "Macedonian Cry" in our hymns that have themes of missions.

The Holy Spirit sent Paul three days journey and more than one hundred and forty miles away from Troas to Philippi in order to answer the cry of the man from Macedonia. When Paul arrived at Macedonia, he found no man. His first contact was with a few women who were gathered for prayer. About a mile from the city, the road leading to

8

this city crossed a small river. This is most likely the place of prayer where Paul found these Philippian women. Lydia, a seller of purple, was the first convert of Europe-again a lady and not a man. Men were saved a short while later, according to Acts 16:40.

Paul was constantly harassed by a girl possessed with an unclean spirit. He cast the unclean spirit out of the girl, and when her masters saw that the hope of their gains were gone, they accused Paul before the magistrate. The magistrate then put both Paul and Silas into prison after they were scourged with a whip. This was the very first time Paul met with Gentile persecution. Up to this point all persecution towards the Christians had come from the Jews. Only twice in the book of Acts do we find Gentile hostility towards the gospel. In both cases, someone's financial gain was threatened.

At midnight, Paul and Silas were singing praises unto God for all the prisoners to hear. There was an earthquake that shook the foundation of the prison and broke the bonds of every prisoner. The keeper of the prison was awakened and nearly took his own life. If one prisoner would have escaped, he would have been executed. When Paul convinced him that all remained, the Philippian jailor fell at Paul's feet and said, *Sirs, what must I do to be saved.* The jailor brought God's servants out of the prison and took them into his own house. The Jailor washed the stripes on the backs of Paul and Silas. Paul preached in his home and his entire house were saved and baptized. The next day, the magistrate sent word to release Paul and Silas and they went on their way to found the church at Thessalonica. Paul left Ephesus during his third missionary journey and returned to Macedonia once again. He went to Corinth and from Corinth he returned to Philippi where he kept the Passover-Acts 20:6.

Notice the people who made up the church at Philippi:

- † Lydia- an Asian and an immigrant from Thyatira (Acts 16:14)- an upper class businesswoman.
- † The Jailor- a Roman- a middle class working man.
- † The Damsel- a native Greek from Philippi- a member of the lower class.

The church was perfectly balanced. It was open to all classes and all cultures from every country. So it should be today.

The Crucible

It was here in Philippi that Paul was placed in the crucible of suffering that would forever change his ministry. I believe what happened within the prison cell in Philippi was a defining moment for Paul and his ministry in the years to come. We have more details on this occasion of persecution than any other persecution in the life of Paul. Why? It was a defining moment. Paul was stripped to the waist, tied to a pole and a Roman whip peeled the flesh off his back. He was chained hand and foot to the floor of a hard, cold prison. His body was still in a state of shock. Chained as he was, there was no way to get comfortable. The pain of the beating would have still been agonizing even if he were lying on a soft bed. The midnight hour is upon Paul and Silas. The night is dark. The cell is cold. The pain is excruciating. No one would have blamed Paul if he had quit right there. Paul could have said to himself, "I have preached to the Jews and they have persecuted me. Now the Gentiles have beaten and imprisoned me. I cannot get anything done for God. Serving God is not worth the pain it brings. I have had enough." This is more often than not the attitude of many Christians who are placed into the crucible of a defining moment. Why is it the more bitter Christians become the more enlightened they become?   Everything they say starts like with, "Well you don't know...You can't tell me...Let me tell you...." There is always suffering in service to God. *1 Peter 2:21 For even hereunto were ye called: because Christ also suffered for us, leaving us an example, that ye should follow his steps...* Your light affliction is but for a moment. It is given to birth a spirit of prayer and an attitude of praise that show just how real and how great your God really is. Paul did not quit in that cell. Instead prayer and praise were offered unto to God at midnight. They praised God in their sufferings.   They gave glory to God for their afflictions. Paul had a great attitude. We must always strive to maintain a good attitude because you and I usually do not recognize a defining moment until the moment has passed.

Every good Christian will be doing God's work, just like Paul, and somebody is going to have a fit about it. It may be the world without, or the church within, and your first time certainly will not be your last time. You are going to be tempted to give in to despair and

11

defeat. We always talk about Paul the missionary, but rarely do we speak of the keys to Paul's success as a missionary. I believe the secret to Paul's success was his prayer life and his attitude of praise. Consider Paul the prayer warrior. Paul records thirty-six prayers in fourteen epistles and sixty times we find him giving praise and thanks to God. Before every major event in the life of our Lord, you find Him first alone in prayer. You can pray the power of God down or you can praise it down. Paul did both. Maybe he sang *"It will be worth it all when we see Jesus"* or *"Hallelujah, What a Savior"* or *"Abide With Me."*

God let Paul sit there in that cell long enough to make a conscious choice about his attitude towards God and His divine will. God wants us to sit in our afflictions so He can see what our attitude really is. This would not be Paul's attitude just in Philippi's prison, but this would be Paul's attitude for life. Paul said in *Philippians 4:11b-13 I have learned, in whatsoever state I am, therewith to be content. I know both how to be abased, and I know how to abound: every where and in all things I am instructed both to be full and to be hungry, both to abound and to suffer need. I can do all things through Christ which strengtheneth me.* "Have" means that he learned this lesson in the past. He learned this lesson in a prison cell in Philippi. There is not a greater example than the prison at Philippi. Philippi was the great trial of affliction that solidified how Paul would respond to suffering and persecution for the rest of his life. You can see this as you read the personal testimony of Paul's sufferings in 2 Corinthians 12. Also, Paul would use what he learned in Philippi to exhort other churches, such as Thessalonica, as well. *2 Thessalonians 1:3-5 We are bound to thank God always for you, brethren, as it is meet, because that your faith groweth exceedingly, and the charity of every one of you all toward each other aboundeth; So that we ourselves glory in you in the churches of God for your patience and faith in all your persecutions and tribulations that ye endure: Which is a manifest token of the righteous judgment of God, that ye may be counted worthy of the kingdom of God, for which ye also suffer...* God's greatest works have always come from great sufferings. In Acts 4, after he was beaten, Peter rejoiced that he was counted worthy to suffer such shame. We often think of the midnight hour as a time of great darkness and despair. We refer to it as a low point in our life. By definition, midnight is the beginning of a new day. Paul praised God and prayed at midnight because a brand new day was upon him. A better day was upon him. Paul's attitude in prison determined his fruitfulness when free. The jailor would be saved and his whole house. Paul would finally meet the man of Macedonia from his vision.

Paul's second missionary journey could have been over before it started, and there would have never been a third or a fourth journey. What if Paul had not rejoiced or sang praises to God? The work of Christ could have died in that prison cell. After Philippi, Paul was sent to Thessalonica, Corinth, Ephesus, Colosse and Rome- much larger churches and often considered his greatest works. We have only one New Testament epistle written to the churches from Paul's first journey. That is the book of Galatians, which was written to a group of

13

churches. Almost every first missionary journey church is mentioned only once in the Bible. If there had been no Philippi, there would be no churches in Ephesus, Rome, Corinth, Thessalonica, Berea or Nicopolis. We would not need Titus or Timothy, for they would not have gone to Crete, Dalmatia or Ephesus. Paul's great works- the churches of Rome, Ephesus, Corinth, Colosse and Thessalonica- were dependent on this small work. Philippi was the one who paid to send Paul to start the other churches. They sent to his necessity twice at Thessalonica, once at Corinth and again at Rome. We often preach (and it is true) that a simple act of disobedience changes your life. We usually cite Adam and Eve as our example. However, a simple act of obedience can change your life for the better and have far reaching rewards as well. The action of your attitude can change your life too.

Your uplook determines your outlook. I learned this first hand when some time ago, my family and I were in eastern Europe visiting some of our missionaries. While we were there, the word got out to friends of the missionary that we were going to be in the area, so we were invited to Romania for a couple of days. I preached in a Romanian church on a Wednesday night. As we came into the church, a man walked up to our Serbian missionary and began to speak to him. His name is Dan Gavra. You could tell immediately that this guy was the happy guy in the church. Dan is the one who is up when everyone else is down. He is the one who sees that every cloud has a silver lining. He is most certainly a nuisance to those with the martyr's complex in the church. He is certainly not understood by the pessimists. There were several prayer cards of different missionaries in his Bible. He pulled one out only to reveal that it was a prayer card of the missionary who brought us to the church. He wanted him to know that he had been praying for him. I met his wife and teenage daughter. They were a sweet family. I learned that Dan drove the church bus. This was somewhat unusual because Dan only has one leg. He walks on what we used to call polio crutches. Some might call them walking crutches. I was so impressed with Dan's spirit, attitude and service that later that evening I asked the missionary to tell me about Dan. He told me this story.

First, we were in a group with some other folks from the church and they explained a little about communism to us. There was three brands of communism in eastern Europe and Asia. There is the old ten nation Yugoslavian type. This was the mildest. Then there was a more cruel oppressive form of communism under the old USSR, which was controlled by Russia. The third brand of communism is Romanian, which is by far the worst and the most cruel. No one owns anything. For instance, if you have a chicken, it belongs to "the people." You cannot have the eggs. You cannot eat the chicken. You must feed the people's chicken, but since the chicken cannot be equally divided amongst six million Romanians, you just keep feeding the chicken until it dies and let the eggs rot. The same goes for the milk of a cow. We met a lady my wife's age who had never seen a bottle of soda or a bar of chocolate until communism fell in the 1990's. There would be food on the shelves in the store, but no money to buy it with. Then there would be money, but no food to buy. Everyone stole and starved except the rich. In communism, everyone is equal, but some are more equal than others. The people had no concept of the world outside of Romania. From 1965 until the Romanian revolution in 1989, they only had state news and lived by the strict Soviet-bloc standards. This was the world of the happy Dan Gavra.

Dan was in the city of Timisoara. Timisoara was one of the cities in which the Romanian revolution against communism would take place. The good news in those days was that the gospel was still present, though it traveled in hushed tones in barns, small apartments and alleyways. A local pastor by the name of Laszlo Tokes was becoming a threat to the Communist leaders. He was preaching liberty from sin and tyranny because he believed the gospel frees you from both. The communists wanted to run this pastor out of the city. For the first time a group of believers gathered to pray and to take a public stand against the communist regime. Dan was not a member of Laszlo Tokes congregation, but he and his girlfriend along with many other believers came to show their support. At the end of the day the crowd began to leave, but a few remained behind. Those that remained were strong in heart and faith, and they did not want such a special day to be over. So they went and bought candles and stood on the steps of the large Cathedral at the end of the Timisoara square. They were sending a message to the communists. The communists said God was dead. Their response was that God was alive. The cathedral was a tangible object that said God is not dead. The people began to shout for

Romania to wake up and cast down communism. More protestors came, and soon the military came. They took a Romanian flag and cut the symbol of communism out of its center. They began to wave it as they marched through the square. The Secret Police lined up across from the crowd of peaceful protestors and showed their weapons. The people shouted for them not to shoot, but they did anyway. Dan was shot in the leg, and his girlfriend was shot in the stomach. Some of the protestors drug Dan off to a hospital for treatment. The communists were searching the hospitals, looking for the wounded protestors of the state. A Christian nurse hid Dan and continued to care for him. His girlfriend was thrown on a pile of dead bodies and burned. Dan never saw her again. The revolt started an uprising all across Romania. Ceausescu, the communist dictator, fled the country but was captured and convicted on Christmas day. He and his family were executed by a firing squad. Communism collapsed in Romania.

You can still see the bullet holes in the buildings of Timisoara square. They took our family for a walk down that square, and we stood on the steps of the cathedral, where Dan had stood more than twenty years earlier. Do you know what Dan says about losing his leg? He said, "I didn't mind losing my leg. I got to light the first candle." Dan, like the apostle Paul, had a great attitude in affliction. He was placed in the crucible of a defining moment, and his life has never been the same. Dan will never live in a fine house. He will never have near the money that people in America have, but he has every good and perfect gift from above. He has salvation. He has a Christian family.

He has a place of service for his Savior. He is far happier than most Christians and many pastors in our country will ever be. Serving Christ is award enough for him. It was for Paul, too. Paul would later say to the church at Rome, *Romans 8:18 For I reckon that the sufferings of this present time are not worthy to be compared with the glory which shall be revealed in us.*

I wonder how many of the great things of God have died in a prison cell just like Philippi, and they all died for the want of a good attitude in affliction that says as John did in *Revelation 4:11 Thou art worthy, O Lord, to receive glory and honour and power: for thou hast created all things, and for thy pleasure they are and were created.* The history of the true church is filled with the testimonies of those like Dan Gavra and Paul who God divinely placed into the crucible of suffering in order to produce a greater ministry and a greater glory on behalf of the Lord Jesus Christ. Prisons have produced far better Christians than any palace.

The Content

Philippians is one of Paul's many epistles (letters). In fact, Polycarp, the bishop of Smyrna, wrote a letter to Philippi in the early second century and made note that Paul had written several letters to Philippi. Demetrius, an ancient Greek literary critic, wrote on one occasion: "Everyone reveals his own soul in his letters. In every other form of composition it is possible to discern the writer's character, but in none so clearly as epistolary." We feel we know the Apostle Paul so well because we have so many of his letters in the word of God. On the other hand, we sometimes struggle with Paul's letters because we have only one side of a two-sided conversation. It is often like listening to someone talking on the telephone. We only hear half the conversation. This letter to Philippi was different from all the others in its eternal inspiration and preservation. This was Paul's perfect letter to Philippi. Letters put us in touch with people in a personal way. God's Word is a personal letter to every man. This letter is not one sided for you and I because God is still speaking to the church today. You and I are the other side of the conversation. We may have both a full and a clear understanding with God in heaven through the Word of truth and the Spirit of truth. For thousands of years letters have been basically written in the same format. Almost all letters have this structure:

- ❖ Greeting
- ❖ Prayer for the good health of those to whom the letter is written
- ❖ Thanksgiving to the gods
- ❖ Special message
- ❖ Specific salutation and personal greetings from those surrounding the author

There is a letter from a Roman soldier called Apion written to his father Epimachus. Apion writes to his father from Misenum to let him know he has arrived safely at his new outpost after surviving a stormy voyage. It can be read today two thousand years later in *Selections from the Greek Papyri*. A common man, an unconverted soldier, wrote in the same manner and with the same method that Paul did.

Philippians, like Philemon, reveals a personal side of Paul and a grateful heart. It appears that the church had lost touch with Paul-most likely during his two year imprisonment in Caesarea. Somehow the church got word that Paul was in prison at Rome. Fearing Paul might be in need, they sent once again to meet his needs by the hand of Epaphroditus. Paul wrote from the prison at Rome (AD 64) to the church at Philippi about ten years after he had planted it. It had been about three or four years since he had last visited. Epaphroditus, one of the Philippian elders, had arrived with financial support after nearly losing his life during his journey to find Paul. The Philippians loved Paul and faithfully supported him both prayerfully and financially in his missions work. The church at Philippi had sent financial support to Paul twice at Thessalonica, at least once at Corinth and then again at Rome. They are the only church that has a record of giving to the needs of Paul. Through the giving of the Philippians, Paul provoked the church at Corinth to give to the Jews but we have no record of Corinth ever having done so. This epistle is Paul's thank you letter for their continued and faithful support. Paul's gratitude is expressed repeatedly throughout this epistle.

Paul wrote almost exclusively to deal with some specific strife that arose in the churches. Paul wrote to Corinth the first time because a man was living in sin with his father's wife. He wrote to Corinth the second time to urge for the restoration of the repentant man. He wrote to the Colossians because false prophets were teaching that angels should be worshipped instead of Christ alone. He wrote to the Thessalonians to assure them that they had not missed the Second Coming as some seducers had been propagating. He wrote to the Galatians because they were bewitched into believing that they must be circumcised in order to obtain full salvation.

It appears that two ladies had been at odds (Euodias and Syntyche- Philippians 4:2) who were both beloved and respected by Paul and their church. If their differences were not settled, it would cause division and damage in the days ahead. Paul urged discontented members to set aside their personal animosity and their petty preferences toward each other and to live peaceably.

Paul's letters were written in four groups. Philippians is the first letter in Paul's third group of letters. This group of prison epistles contains Ephesians, Philippians, Colossians and Philemon. Many also believe Hebrews was written by Paul at this time. The actual order of their writing is Philippians, Philemon, Colossians, Ephesians, and Hebrews. Ephesians is canonized first in the New Testament but was actually written second to last if Hebrews was indeed written at this time. The letters to Philemon, the Colossians and the Ephesians were sent at one time. The internal evidence of the Scriptures seems to point that Philippians was the first letter sent, and Hebrews was the last.

Paul wrote it as he was chained to a Roman Praetorian soldier both day and night. Paul was bound, but the Word of God was not bound. Paul certainly infected the emperor's guard with the gospel. Philippians is one the most personal of Paul's letters. Our theme for Philippians is *"Reasons To Rejoice In Christ."* The word "rejoice" is found nineteen times in four short chapters. After Epaphroditus recovered from his illness, Paul sent him back to Philippi with this letter. They had sown temporal things but they were going to reap eternal rewards. Nero was the reigning Caesar but had not yet turned his hatred toward the Christians. Paul had not yet been brought to trial. He sat waiting as the wheels of Roman justice turned slowly.

Philippi surpassed all the other apostolic churches in their liberality towards Paul and their fidelity to the simplicity of the gospel. This church had very small beginnings and never records a great number of converts like some of Paul's other churches, such as Ephesus and Corinth. The population of Philippi is estimated at ten thousand in the first century. They were a small church in a small town that God used in a big way. They were a poor church that proved profitable to God. If Philippi were in existence today, their favorite hymn would probably be *"Little Is Much When God Is In It."* The church at Philippi is a great encouragement to small churches that they may be mightily used by God. They were able to meet the needs of the man who met the needs of nearly all the infant Gentile churches scattered across two continents. It is estimated that the average Independent Baptist church in the United States runs about one hundred forty people. That includes churches that run from five to more than five thousand. The typical church attendance is about one hundred. After three and a half years of both a miracle working and prophetic fulfilling ministry, Jesus left a church of only one hundred twenty in the upper room. All this to say that Philippi represents the average church today.

We have little record of the church at Philippi after the early part of the second century. A few of the early church fathers reference it- Ignatius, Polycarp and Tertullian. As far as post-apostolic history goes there are only two recorded events of Philippi, both of which occurred within a few years of the death of the Apostle John. First, church history bears record that the church at Philippi gave a great reception to Ignatius, the Bishop of Antioch, as he was on his way to Rome to be martyred. The second event was Polycarp's (a disciple of John and the pastor of Smyrna) letter to the Philippians in response to a request they made to him.

There is an old proverb that says, "Blessed is the land that has no history." The message of the proverb is that history is devoted to great changes, wars and crimes. B.H. Carroll said, "The peaceful, happy life has no records." Most of humanity pursues this life and never finds it. A peaceful life will only be found through the Prince of Peace. The church of Philippi had found Jesus Christ and the happiness and peace that only He can bring.

The word "sin" is not mentioned one single time in this book. The flesh is referred to only to be ignored. These were true servants to God and no slaves to sin were found in her hallowed halls. Four times Paul refers to his bonds, but he always causes us to believe that he is more free than the Roman soldier he is chained to.

This letter deals with the believer's state (earthly condition) as opposed to the believer's standing (eternal position). Philippians is the fiftieth of the sixty six books of the Bible. It has four chapters; one hundred four verses; two thousand two words; one question; ninety-six verses of history; and five verses of unfulfilled prophecy. F.B. Meyer said of Philippians that it is "the tenderest Epistle Paul ever wrote." Handley Moule called it "One of the fairest and dearest regions of the book of God."

Chapter 1

Rejoicing In Christ Our Position

Paul's Prologue- Philippians 1:1-2

Philippians 1:1-2 *Paul and Timotheus, the servants of Jesus Christ, to all the saints in Christ Jesus which are at Philippi, with the bishops and deacons: Grace be unto you, and peace, from God our Father, and from the Lord Jesus Christ.*

As we have already stated by way of introduction, this letter is clearly a letter written to friends. It is one of Paul's most personal letters. There is neither chiding nor rebuke from Paul to Philippi. It has already been mentioned that the word sin is not even found in this letter.

We know that Paul used different men to dictate his letters to because of his poor vision. It appears that, as Timothy pens the words, Paul speaks through the inspiration of the Holy Spirit. Timothy was also used to help pen 2 Corinthians, Colossians, 1 & 2 Thessalonians and Philemon. Luke was Paul's faithful companion, physician and fellow laborer in Christ. Paul used Luke to pen Hebrews and other books, but a young preacher needed the lessons of Philippians far more than a companion. It is fitting that Timothy would do so. It would be a good lesson for Timothy to learn to rejoice in the oftentimes lonely office of a bishop and also to be thankful for the care the church would bestow on him at Ephesus. Paul brings Timothy alongside of him to instruct Timothy as well as Philippi. Putting the pen to Paul's letters would provide Timothy with valuable insight in dealing with people. Older preachers should make it a habit to disciple their preacher boys along the way. Moses had Joshua. Elijah passed his mantle to Elisha. Paul instructed Timothy and Titus. Leaders need to reproduce themselves. Leaders reproduce themselves by investing in those who will stand in their place. This is great wisdom for parents and grandparents as well as pastors.

Paul did not claim his apostolic authority when writing to the church at Philippi. He described himself as a servant. Paul had to defend his apostolic authority when writing to the churches in Galatia and Corinth. He did not need to defend his office to his friends at Philippi. Paul wrote to all the saints at Philippi. He did not write to a clique or a group that felt superior to those they considered inferior. All of the Bible is for all of God's people. God and His Word are no respecter of persons and neither was Paul. It has been said that all of humanity can be classified into two groups-"the saints" and "the ain'ts."

Notice in verse one that there are servants and there are saints. This is a twin description for believers. Not all saints are servants, but all saints should be servants. A servant is free to come and go but slaves are the possessions of their masters. Christians are in a unique position. We are in the position of bondservants- Exodus 21:1-6 and Deuteronomy 15:12-18. Bondservants are those who were slaves for a time (typically six years) but then became free to choose whether or not to continue in the service of a righteous master or go out on their own. If one chose to remain in the service of his master, he retained the provision and blessings of his master's house- including his wife and children. You only kept the benefits by becoming a bondservant. Once you chose to become a bondservant, you stood before a door and your ear was bored through with an aul, and a gold earring was put in the ear. You were marked as the master's servant for life. We were the slaves and servants of sin, but then Christ set us free. He wants us to choose to serve Him. All the blessings and provision of the Christian life are found in service to Christ in the Master's house. You will never know a true Christian family outside the boundaries of being a bondservant for Jesus Christ.

Paul makes it clear that he is the possession of Christ. He is the purchased property (redeemed) of Christ. Physically, Paul was the prisoner of Caesar in Rome, but Paul saw himself as Christ's servant even though he was chained to a Roman soldier while sitting in a Roman cell and later a hired house. Four times in the first chapter Paul refers to his bonds- verses seven, thirteen, fourteen, and sixteen. Paul only considered himself the "prisoner of the Lord" and never the prisoner of Nero. He did not consider himself under the power of man.

He knew he was in the will of God. When Paul testified of Christ in Jerusalem, the Lord appeared to him and told him to be of good cheer and to know that he would also testify of Jesus in Rome also- Acts 23:11. Great and wondrous works have been accomplished in bonds. Paul wrote inspired epistles and started churches in bonds- including the church at Rome. Marco Polo wrote his book *Travels* while in bonds. Who could forget Bedford prison where John Bunyan wrote *Pilgrim's Progress?* Christ owned Paul, and Paul would have it no other way nor would he see himself any other way. Paul was fully yielded to Christ and his joy in his bonds is eternal evidence.

Paul and Timothy claimed the highest of all titles-servants of Jesus Christ. Can you write that statement after your name? Would God the Father write that statement after your name? That should be the heart's desire of all Christians. This titled will be claimed only by doing our daily duty. Unfortunately, many have the heart of James and John. They are always striving to see who is the greatest in the kingdom instead of simply striving to serve their Lord to the best of their ability. There is an old Latin saying *Illi servire est regnare-* to be His slave is to be a king. Indeed, Peter tells us that God has made us kings and priests unto Himself.

Service was the sum and substance, the ultimate of Paul's whole life, for this was his conception of the Christian life. ~Lehman Strauss

Would you be a saint indeed? Then live 'in Christ Jesus' as your King (Christ), and in Jesus in all the human relationship of daily life (Jesus). Let Him be your atmosphere and environment, your protection from the assaults of evil from without, and the sweet fragrance which will exhale through the inner sanctuary of your nature, in speech and act.
~F.B. Meyer

A saint is not just a Christian who is departed and gone to heaven. All the redeemed are saints in their days on the earth. Paul wrote to "all" the saints. He does not exclude anyone. There are no classes in Christianity. There is no caste system. The ground is level at the foot of the cross and Jesus said that of all who came to Him, He would in no wise cast anyone out. He includes all who are saved. The word saint simply means "sanctified one" or "one who is set apart by God." It is the same word as holy. Saints are *holy ones.* This is God's title for all God's children. We are God's property set apart to be different for God's use. One who is sanctified or set apart is different from another. Christians are not better than non-Christians, but we are certainly better off. We are different.

The priests were different or "set apart" for a special service from the congregation. The Holy Place of the tabernacle was different from any other place in the temple or the land of Israel. The Jews were holy as a nation. They were different from all other nations on the face of the earth. So it is to be with Christians. All we think, say or do is to be different from the world we live in. You do not have to be sinless to be a saint, though saints "sin less." Paul did not call the Philippians saints because they were sinless. In fact, there was dissension in the assembly between two women that he later addresses. Holy people are often unholy. Saints often behave unsaintly. Our sanctification is not complete until we reach heaven. We all have room for improvement, but anything or anyone that is set apart for the use of God is holy. The pots and pans of the tabernacle were probably battered and worn by being drug all over the wilderness for forty years, but even they were called holy vessels. They simply washed the dust and dirt of the desert off of them and continued to use them even unto the days of Solomon. God will not use a filthy vessel, but He will use any vessel that has been cleansed through confession of sins. He will use battered and scarred vessels. Those vessels may not have looked holy, but they were holy. Why? Because they were set apart. They were different. So it is with us.

We serve a holy God. A holy God demands a holy people. One of the great errors of the modern perversions of scripture is that they remove the holiness of God. They simply remove the word holy as if God never was. All the places that say holy men, women, angels, saints, and countless other descriptions are simply deleted as if God could never make anything holy or set it apart for His honor and glory. If you remove God's holiness, you have no need of God, His salvation or eternal life through His Son for there is no standard of righteousness to go by. Notice a few of the things God calls holy in the Bible.

✝ Our God is a thrice holy God- Isaiah 6:3; Revelation 4:8.

✝ Our holy Saviour- Acts 4:27, 30.

✝ The indwelling Spirit of God is the Holy Ghost- Acts 1:8.

✝ Our Bible is holy- Romans 1:2.

✝ Brethren are holy- 1 Thessalonians 5:27; Hebrews 3:1.

✝ The church is a holy priesthood- 1 Peter 2:5.

✝ We have a holy calling- 2 Timothy 1:9.

✝ Jesus presents us to our Father "holy and unblameable and unreproveable in his sight"- Colossians 1:22.

✝ John called the New Jerusalem the "holy city"- Revelation 21:2.

Peter admonishes that in view of the knowledge of the coming of the Lord we should live holy unto God. *2 Peter 3:11-12 Seeing then that all these things shall be dissolved, what manner of persons ought ye to be in all holy conversation and godliness, Looking for and hasting unto the coming of the day of God, wherein the heavens being on fire shall be dissolved, and the elements shall melt with fervent heat?*

Paul writes to saints who are *in* Christ but living *at* Philippi. The epistles (letters) of Paul contain the words *in Christ Jesus* forty-eight times, *in Christ* occurs thirty-four times and *in the Lord* fifty times. The words "in Christ" are among the most important words in all of the New Testament. Wherever they are found, the saints are the epicenter of those words. There are great theological words all through the New Testament that describe our salvation- words like propitiation, reconciliation, redemption, adoption, atonement, justification, sanctification, glorification and others. Those words describe some specific attribute of our salvation. The little word "in" is the one word that has the power to describe the fullness of our salvation like no other single word can. To be saved is to be in Christ.

Paul writes to all the saints, but he specifically addresses the bishops and deacons. The words bishop and elder are used interchangeably throughout the New Testament. The word bishop describes the office of the pastor. The word elder acknowledges the pastor fulfilling his office. Deacons are also mentioned by Paul. These men were servants not lords. They attended to the secular service of the church keeping the elders free to search the Scriptures and be given to prayer.

Here again we find Paul's familiar greeting of grace and peace. Grace was the western (occidental) greeting and peace was the eastern (oriental) greeting. Grace and peace are twin sisters and a greater greeting will not be found than the beauty found in the words "grace and peace." The old Baptist preacher Herbert Lockyer wrote that "grace and peace are both the root and the fruit of all Christian experience." Grace is the Greek greeting. Peace is the Hebrew greeting. Paul used the greetings of both and yoked them together in nearly all of his epistles. It showed that the wall of partition was removed between the Jews and the Greeks in order to reveal the church of Jesus Christ. The church is one without difference to either Jew or Greek in Christ Jesus.

In the early church spiritual gifts had definite ranks and priorities, but grace was for all men. The Greeks said "grace" and meant "have a good day." When a Christian says "grace" we are saying "have a good eternity." For the Greek, grace also was considered a favor done for a friend. For the Christian grace is more. God showed us His favour when we were His enemies by sinning against Him. God showed favour and gave His only begotten Son as a ransom for all. The Greeks would do a favor for a friend but never an enemy. God showed favor to His enemies through Jesus Christ our Lord.

Peace always follows grace. Grace must come first. The order can never be reversed. There is only peace to those who have first known grace. There is no peace without the grace of God that brings salvation. There is peace *with* God. That is my position with God. I am at peace with God through the blood of the cross. I have the peace *of* God that comes from living in obedience to His Word. Peace with God is my standing. The peace of God is my state. The former is my eternal condition. The latter is my earthly condition. God gives to His people a peace that passes all understanding that keeps our hearts and minds in Christ Jesus.

Peace is lacking in some Christian homes for no other reason than that grace is lacking in the Christian's hearts. ~Lehman Strauss

Grace and peace both come...*from God our Father, and from the Lord Jesus Christ.* God is the God of all grace and peace so we only obtain them from Him. It is worthy to note that Paul mentions the Savior's name more than forty times in this brief epistle. That is once for every two to three verses. It is actually very characteristic of all the New Testament writers. It provokes us to ask ourselves, "How often do I mention the name of Jesus in my daily conversation?" I am afraid if most Christians answered honestly we would be shocked and ashamed upon our examination. The trouble is that the name of Jesus does not fit the conversation of many who claim to be His disciples today. A life lived for Jesus will speak often of Jesus.

Paul has mentioned both the Father and the Son, but do not think he has neglected the Holy Spirit. Paul was a Trinitarian. Where is the Holy Spirit in these verses? The Holy Spirit was in the saints at Philippi. He indwelled them and filled them. When Paul wrote to the saints in Christ, he was making clear mention of the presence of the Holy Spirit as well. Without the Holy Spirit no one would be in Christ.

Paul's Praise- Philippians 1:3-8

Philippians 1:3-8 *I thank my God upon every remembrance of you, Always in every prayer of mine for you all making request with joy, For your fellowship in the gospel from the first day until now; Being confident of this very thing, that he which hath begun a good work in you will perform it until the day of Jesus Christ: Even as it is meet for me to think this of you all, because I have you in my heart; inasmuch as both in my bonds, and in the defence and confirmation of the gospel,*

34

ye all are partakers of my grace. For God is my record, how greatly I long after you all in the bowels of Jesus Christ.

Paul now begins with a word of praise. This may seem a strange thing to say, but praise and persecution may always sit beside each other. There can always be praise even though we may be imprisoned in some way. Paul found a reason to rejoice in his bonds. When Paul sought within his heart for a reason to rejoice in his bonds, Philippi immediately came to his mind. This was a church that Paul had nothing but good things to say about it. The authenticity of Paul's praise is that God inspired it to be eternally recorded. It should be the desire of every church to hear nothing but good from God.

Thankfulness and gratefulness are yoked together when Paul remembers Philippi. Thank God for good memories in the church! Every Christian should be able to talk for hours about the good memories God has given them through the years. They are a small part of the reward for faithfulness. Paul's interest in Philippi did not cease when he left them. In fact, as we shall see in the following verses, his interest and love for them only grew to greater heights.

Remember this is the same Philippi where Paul was mocked, imprisoned and beaten. Some of our darkest hours may be yoked with some of our sweetest memories. This is also where Lydia, the first convert of Europe, was saved. A young girl was delivered from the power of an unclean spirit. Paul and Silas sang and praised God at midnight and saw God deliver them from their chains in a miraculous way. The Philippian jailor and his whole house were saved. You can have some of your fondest memories in spite of some of life's darkest hours. My father's pastor, Pastor William B. Mussellman, always said, "Accentuate the positive. Don't dwell on the negative." That is sage advice.

Paul's thanks for Philippi is remarkable. Paul uses the terms "all", "always", and "every." These are the highest words of thanks. Paul never said anything like this to any of the other churches he started so far as Biblical record is concerned. He certainly loved them, but he could never say anything like this of them. Thank God for Philippi! Words such as these ought to be said of someone. I remember the first time I preached a pastor's fellowship meeting. I grew up listening to these men of God preach for my father when I was a boy. Most of them had been in the ministry and serving in the same churches for more years that I had been alive. I did not know what to preach. I came across this verse used it for my text. I thanked them for the memories I had of each of them and what they had invested in me. I also blamed them if there was error in my doctrine or poor ability in my preaching as they were the ones who had raised me!

What a tremendous statement Paul makes here in verse four! Every time that Paul prayed, he prayed for Philippi! Paul said that he remembered them only with joy. There was not a single negative emotion when Paul went to the throne of grace on behalf of Philippi. As a pastor, there are people that I dearly love, yet when I pray for them it is always with grief and anguish, because I am burdened by the

36

actions of their sinful lives. Every pastor needs someone to pray for that only brings joy to the heart and to the mind.

It has been said that the best way to remember someone is to remember them in prayer before God. Our Lord lives to intercede for us and so also should the church intercede for each other. The pastor should pray for his people and the people for their pastor. Every teacher ought to pray for their students and the students for their teachers. We prove our devotion to God and each other by praying for each other. The distance between church members would be shortened if it were filled with love and prayer. Lancelot Andrewes was the chief scholar and translator for the King James Bible. He spent five hours a day in personal devotions. Much of that time was spent pouring his heart out for those he loved. Christians would have better memories of each other if we spent more time in prayer for each other. There is an old story of a nurse who taught a very disgruntled man to pray. His prayers changed him into a man of joy. The nurse told the man that our hands are a good lesson on how to pray for those we love. Each finger reminded her of someone. Her thumb was nearest to her, so it reminded her to pray for those closest to her. The second finger was used for pointing, and it stood for all her teachers in school and in the hospital. The third finger was the tallest, and it stood for the leaders in every sphere of her life. The fourth finger was is the weakest finger, and it reminded her to pray for those who were in trouble or in pain. Her little finger was her smallest finger and the least important.

The nurse said that reminded her that she herself was the least and the last to be prayed for.

Paul and the Philippians had not seen each other in ten years, but they had never been out of fellowship. They had continued in their fellowship by prayer and giving of thanks for each other. They were always together in heart, mind, and spirit before the throne of God. Churches often do not see their missionaries for years at a time, yet when they return to us it seems as if they were never gone. We have been together all along in our fellowship of the gospel.

It should be noticed what a large place the words "fellowship" and "gospel" are given in this epistle. The word fellowship is used five times and the word gospel is used eight times in these few chapters. The word fellowship that is used here comes from the same word that was used for the marriage bond. Their fellowship was powerful, binding and unbreakable. Their fellowship was likened to a covenant relationship that could never be destroyed. What could hold such a bond between Paul and Philippi? The gospel was their bond. This is a sweet picture of being joint heirs with Christ and also a reminder of our eternal security. Theirs was a fellowship of the Spirit- Philippians 2:1. Happy is the church that knows both the fellowship and the fruit of the Holy Spirit!

The word fellowship here has a preposition attached to it. It makes the stronger and gives it more meaning. When we think of fellowship, we think of being "with" someone in some way. Here the word fellowship means "being all wrapped up together." It reminds us of what the Bible says about the relationship between Jacob and Benjamin. Simeon said that Jacob's life was bound up with the life of the lad (Benjamin). Abigail used similar words when she spoke with David...*the soul of my lord shall be bound in the bundle of life with the LORD thy God; and the souls of thine enemies, them shall he sling out, as out of the middle of a sling.* Paul's life and the life of the church at Philippi were bound up in the life of Jesus Christ. They were bound up together in His person and His work. The strongest and most united churches are those that are bound together in Jesus Christ. Jesus is the glue that cements the church together.

An assembly of saints walking together in the fear of the Lord, exercised about holding for the Word of Life to the unsaved, is likely to know more of real fellowship than a company of believers occupied chiefly with their own affairs, their own blessings-all about themselves. ~Dr. Henry Ironside

I love verse six and often quote it. Paul begins with confidence. Paul has no doubt. He has all the assurance in the world when it comes to the promises of God. God's promises are the root and the strength of our faith. God will perform that which He has promised. God's promises never fall apart. The word confident here is the Greek word *peitho.* This word is translated in the New Testament in nine different English words for a total of fifty-three times.

- Persuade- 22 times
- Trust- 10 times
- Confidence- 9 times
- Obey- 7 times
- Assure, believe, agree, yield, and make one's friend- 1 time in each usage

The words that Paul uses for "begun" and "until the day of Jesus Christ" are technical words in the Greek that signify the beginning and the ending of a sacrifice. A good work is one that begins at Calvary with the first coming of Christ. When Christ comes for His bride, His sacrificial work in our lives will be complete. Our redemption, sanctification and glorification will be complete. Between the time of our salvation and the time of the Lord's return, every saint is to be a living sacrifice unto God. When Christ returns, He will return as King of kings and Lord of lords. It is customary in any monarchial system for the servants of the king to present their king with gifts at his coming. No gift will bring more joy to our King than for His saints to present themselves unto Him as living sacrifices. Spurgeon had preached on this verse and at the close of his sermon he heard one crying at the altar, "Lord, make a good job of me! Lord, make a good job of me!"

This verse teaches us that nothing is lacking on God's part or ability to bring about the full work He has elected to do in the life of every single believer. The final condition of every believer will be to stand complete and perfect in Jesus Christ. The soul of the saint is not a lost or broken stream in the desert. It flows from the life of Jesus beginning with salvation and will be sustained until we stand before Him complete.

God has the privilege of inhabiting eternity, thus God can see the finished work of our lives, while to us it is an unfinished work and a glass through which we can only see darkly- 1 Corinthians 13:13. There is a story of an artist who had a great picture in his mind. He was convinced it would his greatest masterpiece. He began working on his canvas with all the of the drab colors and grays that would make up the background. A friend of his came in unnoticed as the artist worked with great enthusiasm. When he realized he was not alone, he turned and saw his friend and asked him what he thought. His friend laughed and said, "Why, to be frank, I don't think much of it. It seems to me to be only a great daub." The artist told his friend, "You cannot see what is going to be there. I can." This is a good illustration of how God sees us. He does not see us only now. He sees what we will be when He has finished His work in our lives as He makes us the praise of His glory. This is also a good lesson for the church. A church will have less strife if it can look beyond some present disappointments and get a small glimpse of what we will be when God is done. God remembers our frame that we are but dust as He molds us into a masterpiece. The church should be as gracious to each other.

The word "meet" is an old English Elizabethan word. It was used commonly in the days when the Bible was translated. We do not use this word today in the same connotation. The word meet is exactly the

41

same word as righteous. God made Adam a help meet. God made Eve "just right" for Adam. Paul was saying that it was right for him to think of them often because they were a people that were dear to his heart. They were dear to Paul's heart because both Paul and Philippi had a heart for the same things. They were in unity being consecrated to the same end. They were one in mind, purpose and life in Christ. It is much the same as a husband and wife. There are two physical bodies, but there is to be one person in unity, spirit, will, purpose and character.

Paul made defence of the gospel. The word "defence" is the Greek word *apologia*. Apologetics is the defence of the gospel. Some preachers are known as great "apologists." There always those who preach another gospel. We defend the gospel by denouncing false gospels and proclaiming the simple truth of the gospel. Paul confirmed the gospel. The word confirmed here means "to build with strength within." To confirm the gospel is to exhort, edify and encourage Christians in the gospel's truth and task. He made sure that the gospel that was taught was the same gospel that was delivered to him by the Lord. Paul had not changed the gospel.

The Philippians were partakers of Paul's grace. They shared the gift of grace with Paul. They shared the common salvation (Jude 3) and had obtained like precious faith (2 Peter 1:1). Paul preached to them, and they were saved. They also were partakers of the work of grace. They supported Paul so that he could preach the gospel to others. The gospel is both a gift and a task. Alexander Maclaren used to say that the church is a workshop and not a dormitory. We do not receive the gospel and then wait for the coming of the Lord while sitting idly by. We must be partakers of the work of grace.

Not only were they partakers of the work of grace by financially and prayerfully supporting Paul, they would also be partakers of the reward of grace. This truth was taught by the our Lord as well. *Matthew 10:41 He that receiveth a prophet in the name of a prophet shall receive a prophet's reward; and he that receiveth a righteous man in the name of a righteous man shall receive a righteous man's reward.* Every member of every true church should have some place in the work of grace. Look at all the women who helped the Lord Jesus on the earth. Look at the list of those servants in Romans 16. The least of all saints may join the chiefest of the apostles by helping them in their labors. Not every church was a partaker of Paul's grace. Some were partakers of his sufferings (Corinth) and inheritance (Colosse), but it appears that only Philippi was a partaker of Paul's grace. Other churches were ungrateful, but Philippi never was.

The word "record" is the Greek word *martus*. *Martus* is used as the word witness twenty-nine times, martyr three times and as the word record two times. God was keeping a record of all that Paul was doing and going through. God was Paul's witness that Paul truly longed to see the Philippians again.

The word bowels simply means "inward parts." The word *splagchna* here was the word the Greeks used to describe the upper intestines, the heart, the liver and the lungs. The Greeks believed the bowels were the inward seat of the emotions. This word means "tender feelings." The Greeks were right. Paul felt a longing for their presence. When a boy or girl is in love, they have butterflies in their stomach not their head. The presence of a young girl will make the heart of a young man to race. When we have sorrow, we say that we have an emptiness inside or a pit in our stomach. We feel within our bowels.

Paul yearned for these Philippians with the same love and longing that he had for Christ. Here is another great word of praise for this church. Not only were they mentioned with joy in every prayer, but Paul missed them as much as he missed Jesus Christ. I do not know of higher words of praise in the New Testament than Paul's words of praise for Philippi.

Paul has praised Philippi but the source of praise and rejoicing is always found in Jesus Christ. All commentators but one claim joy as the theme of this book. Joy is found nineteen times. Jesus Christ is mentioned over forty times in four chapters. The Philippians and the church today have a reason to rejoice, but it is always found in Jesus Christ. The source of all joy stems from the root of Christ.

Paul's Prayer- Philippians 1:9-11

Philippians 1:9-11 *And this I pray, that your love may abound yet more and more in knowledge and in all judgment; That ye may approve things that are excellent; that ye may be sincere and without offence till the day of Christ; Being filled with the fruits of righteousness, which are by Jesus Christ, unto the glory and praise of God.*

Here is another of Paul's great prayers. This has been called Paul's "love-prayer." Brotherly love is more than emotion or sentiment. It is the love of God that moves to action on behalf of those in need. True love does not simply pity those in need. It seeks to meet the needs. *1 John 3:18 My little children, let us not love in word, neither in tongue; but in deed and in truth.* It is good to ask ourselves if our prayers meet the criteria of love.

Paul did not just tell the church he was praying for them. He told them how and what he was praying for them. This is a great lesson as well. People are more likely to believe you are praying for them if they know how you are praying for them and in what manner you are praying on their behalf. One of the biggest lies we tell in the church is "I'm praying for you." Here, Paul gives us a list of how to pray for people. Paul made five requests for the Philippians in his prayers for them:

1. That their love would increase in knowledge and judgment
2. That they would approve excellent things
3. That they would be sincere
4. That they would be without offense until the return of the Lord
5. That they would be filled with the fruits of righteousness for God's praise and glory

Paul prayed that their love would abound more and more in knowledge and judgment. The word "abound" is the verb form of the noun "abundance." An abundance is an exceeding measure above the ordinary. Paul prayed that the Lord would enlarge their capacity and measure for love above what was common to common men. He wanted the Philippians to love Jesus Christ more today than they did yesterday. Love is the greatest of all Christian virtues- 1 Corinthians 13:13. It is the greatest and most important of all of Christ's commands- Matthew 22:36-40. God has made every provision for every Christian to abound in love. It is not only Paul's prayer for the Philippians. It is the prayer of Christ for His church. Notice the words of John: *1 John 3:14-15 We know that we have passed from death unto life, because we love the brethren. He that loveth not his brother abideth in death. Whosoever hateth his brother is a murderer: and ye know that no murderer hath eternal life abiding in him.* The declaration of God is simple and clear. God is love and life, and you cannot have one without the other.

Where there is not exercise of love there is either no life or no learning. ~F.B. Meyer

Paul prayed that they would increase in knowledge. People know what they love. Many cannot quote a verse of Scripture but they can quote countless and meaningless statistics about their favorite athletes. They can give an endless history of their favorite teams and moments in memorable games. They can talk for hours about their grandchildren and hobbies. Love is the way to knowledge. What do you know? Paul knew Christ. He prayed for the people of Christ to learn more about Christ. The purpose of all of Paul's epistles is that those who knew Christ might know Him better. Paul prayed this for himself as well- Philippians 3:10-11. To know Jesus better is to love Jesus more. Love is sensitive and in tune to the heart and will of those it loves. The better you know Jesus, the greater your love for Christ will be. The more you love Him, the more you will desire to please Him. If you love Jesus and learn more of Him, you will be more in tune with God's will and sensitive to the Holy Spirit's leading. People get lost in the will of God when they begin to lose their knowledge of Christ.

This is the only place in the Bible that uses this particular word for "all judgment." It means "discernment." Paul was saying that our love should abound more and more, but love is not to be blind to those who would take advantage of that love. We are to love all men, but we are not to allow all men to take advantage of our Christianity in order to support their worldliness.   We love all men, but we will not walk with them nor work for them in their evil deeds. We will love all men, but we will not financially support them in their continuing evil. We will continually meet new people. Some we can help. Some we cannot. Some will put a knife in your back moments after you helped them. Paul knew that those in need would be constantly coming to the church for help. Paul prayed that the church would have the discernment to help those who were worthy of help and those who were not.

From where do we derive discernment? Paul tells us in Hebrews that the Bible is the best counsel for discernment. *Hebrews 4:12 For the word of God is quick, and powerful, and sharper than any twoedged sword, piercing even to the dividing asunder of soul and spirit, and of the joints and marrow, and is a discerner of the thoughts and intents of the heart.* The Greek word for discerner is *kritikos,* from which we get our English word "critic." The Bible is the best critic on what is excellent. Paul showed the Corinthians a more excellent way through charity. The Bible will help us approve what is excellent in our work of love. We are to love, but we are not to be naïve in our love.

Love is alert and ever looking for an opportunity to serve others. Blind love is not divine love. True love sharpens our perception to see opportunities for service. ~Lehman Strauss

The word "excellent" is the Greek word *diaphero.* It is the word "differ." It is an extension of judgment. Paul is saying that we must use our best judgment, which as has been afore mentioned, is found in light of the Bible. We are to learn the things that are worthy and approve them by meeting the needs of that which is worthy. There is good and there is best. Excellence does what is best. We do not let our children make decisions until they have learned and matured enough to make wise decisions. Paul prayed that they would grow so that they could have the knowledge to make the most excellent choices of Christian service.

The word "sincere" is the Greek word *sincerus,* which means "without wax." At first glance, this is a puzzling prayer. Why would Paul pray that for the Philippians to be "without wax" until the Lord's return? The word "wax" means "tested by the sun." The porcelain of the old world was highly valued and brought a very high price. Porcelain was very fragile and often cracked when being fired in the kiln. Dishonest sellers filled in the cracks with a pearly white wax, which would pass a casual inspection inside a darkened shop. However, if it was taken outside and held up to the sunlight, the wax would be seen as a dark seam. Honest dealers marked their wares as sincerus- "without wax." Also, when the Romans took over the Greek empire, they came in and conquered by brute force. As a result, many of the great Greek art treasures were destroyed. There is much physical archeological evidence of this fact found even today all throughout Asia Minor. After Rome had conquered her world, she began to gather up the treasures that remained in order to incorporate them into their own culture. The Romans had a great appreciation for the Greek arts. Oftentimes someone buying a vase or sculpture would be deceived into buying something that was broken without realizing it. The unsuspecting purchaser would return home with their treasure and put it on display in an outdoor garden and when the sun fell upon the work of art, they would find wax oozing out of the newly acquired piece of art. They would find that it had been cracked and broken. The seller filled it with wax to in order to put it back together. The wax would melt, and the piece would fall apart once again. Sometimes the wax did not melt or ooze out, but when the sun hit the work of art the crack filled with wax became translucent in the light of the sun. It was obvious they had bought a broken piece of art. Again, reputable art dealers began to label their materials *sincerus*- "without wax." Buyers knew they were buying a pure unbroken work of art. Here is a great lesson for the child of God. One day we will all be judged by the light of the Son. May we live to be found blameless and pure and unbroken before Him. Every life has its blemishes, and we have all experienced brokenness but the Potter has power over the clay. Jeremiah 9 gives us a vivid description of God's abilities as the Master Potter. Paul reminded the church at Rome of this in his epistle to them. *Romans 9:21 Hath not the potter power over the clay, of the same lump to make one vessel unto honour, and another unto dishonour?* Let God make each of us into a new vessel that is pure, holy and blameless in His sight.

"Without offense" refers to something that will cause us to fall. We will all fall from time to time, but it should not be to the point where we fall away. Paul prayed that nothing would "off end" or throw the church at Philippi overboard to be left behind as the rest of Christianity sails on. Those who are offended will drown in their sea of sorrows. Those who hold God's word dear to their heart have the promise of God's peace while sailing across life's stormy sea. *Psalms 119:165 Great peace have they which love thy law: and nothing shall offend them.*

The day of Christ is mentioned for the second time in the first ten verses of this chapter. The coming of Christ is the hope of every believer. It is our purpose for purity. We can face each new day knowing this may be the day of the Lord's return. We must live every day and make every decision in light of the coming of our Lord and Savior Jesus Christ knowing that we will give an account to Him at His return.

The word "fruit" (*karos*) is used eight times in this chapter alone. Paul desired for Philippi to be filled with the fruits of righteousness. Someone once said, "A blighted orchard bearing no fruit is a sorry sight. Sadder still is the fruitless life of a child of God!" The word "fruit" is used in reference to the human body. Christ is called the fruit of Mary's womb in Luke 1:42. The fruit of righteousness cannot be produced in an unsaved individual. The fruit of righteousness is found in those who have been regenerated. They may begin to produce a Christ-like life. An unsaved man produces imitation fruit. People used to often put bowls of wax fruit on display. The fruit looked good, but you could do nothing but look at it. You could not eat it. It had no life. Regenerated people produce true and useful righteousness. Righteousness in the unregenerate is useless and meaningless to God. Christ is the vine, and we are the branches. The branch bears the fruit drawing its life from the vine. The glory of the vine is the fruit. The glory of Christ is the fruit of righteousness displayed in His church.

Paul's Palace- Philippians 1:12-18

Philippians 1:12-18 *But I would ye should understand, brethren, that the things which happened unto me have fallen out rather unto the furtherance of the gospel; So that my bonds in Christ are manifest in all* *the palace, and in all other places; And many of the brethren in the Lord, waxing confident by my bonds, are much more bold to speak the word without fear. Some indeed preach Christ even of envy and strife; and some also of good will: The one preach Christ of contention, not sincerely, supposing to add affliction to my bonds: But the other of love, knowing that I am set for the defence of the gospel. What then? notwithstanding, every way, whether in pretence, or in truth, Christ is preached; and I therein do rejoice, yea, and will rejoice.*

Paul knew that all these things had happened to him so that the gospel would go farther than it had already gone before. Paul is telling the Philippians that Rome may chain him, but they cannot put chains on the gospel. Paul's shackles became the wings of the gospel. *2 Timothy 2:9 Wherein I suffer trouble, as an evil doer, even unto bonds; but the word of God is not bound.* The word "furtherance" is a verb that was used in reference to cutting away trees and undergrowth, and the removing of barriers which hinder the progress of an army. Paul knew that his bonds would rally the troops and the gospel would break all barriers. The enlisted would go forth for their captain with the gospel. Paul's gospel was not shut behind the door of the palace. It was still reaching into all the known world.

William Tyndale made it his life's purpose that every plough boy in England be able to know as much of the Bible as the priests who kept it from them. He appealed to the Bishop of London and wound up having to flee his native England. England sought his head everywhere he fled. Tyndale labored for years as he fled all over Europe all the while producing the Tyndale Bible which was the first English Bible and the forerunner of the King James Bible. Tyndale fled to Germany-Hamburg, Cologne and Worms. Then he went to Antwerp in Belgium. Finally he was caught and martyred. He was only forty-six years old when he died in 1536, but he did not die without leaving the Bible in English for the plough boys of England. It has been said that out of his ashes the gospel sprang forth and was scattered all across the land of his nativity through the hands and lips of one hundred thousand men.

The word "palace" is the word *praetorium*. The palace included Caesar's court. Paul was a prisoner in a pit in the palace prison for a time before he was eventually put on house arrest and allowed to have his own hired house- Acts 28:30. The Roman palace had a Praetorian (Palace) guard. Those guards were not just any guards. They had been put in place by Augustus and were ten thousand strong. Tiberius fortified the palace guard in the city of Rome itself and Vitellius raised their number to sixteen thousand. They were the "best of the best" of Rome's army. They served for a term of twelve years. Eventually their enlistment was extended to sixteen years. At the end of their enlistment they received citizenship and a financial reward. They eventually became the emperor's personal bodyguard. There came a time when the Praetorian guards were nothing less than the makers of kings. They would put into power whoever they wanted for emperor and kept them there by force.

Paul was delivered into the hands of the Praetorian Prefect- chief captain. The left hand of a Roman praetorian soldier was chained to

Paul's right hand. The guard changed every six hours four times a day. Even when Paul was sleeping, he was chained to another man. Paul spoke of himself as bound with chains in Acts 28:20. In Ephesians 6:20, he spoke of himself as an ambassador in chains. He used the same word for chains in both places. It was the short chain which bound a prisoner to a praetorian. We find record of this in the book of Acts: *Acts 28:16 And when we came to Rome, the centurion delivered the prisoners to the captain of the guard: but Paul was suffered to dwell by himself with a soldier that kept him.* Paul never considered himself a prisoner but an ambassador of Christ. He represented the person of Christ and the message of the gospel but not himself. His work was being done whether bond or free so he was rejoicing whether bond or free. He speaks of this in chapter four. Paul was preaching Christ in the very palace of Nero. He was able to preach to all who came to see him. *Acts 28:30 And Paul dwelt two whole years in his own hired house, and received all that came in unto him...*I am sure that not all believed. There were probably many guards who mocked, disrupted and criticized Paul's words as he spoke with others of Christ. There was probably some cruel Roman praetorian that disrupted Paul as he tried to sleep attempting to cause weariness to his flesh and perhaps even test his faith to see if he would lose his cool. Ignatius, the bishop of Antioch, was also brought to Rome to be martyred. He described himself as fighting day and night with those guards as fighting with ten leopards. Ignatius said that the kinder he was to the guards the worse they treated him.

Paul said that he took pleasure in his infirmities- 2 Corinthians 12:10. The words "take pleasure" mean "to think well." Paul had a good attitude in bad times. Paul could not help these men through complaint or self-pity. That is shallow Christian living. His contentment and consistency brought rough men with rough ways tenderly to Christ. Paul was faithful and ceased not to pray nor to preach. Some of these guards looked over Paul's shoulder as these very words were being penned by Timothy. They probably sneered and jeered. I wonder how many were converted by his rejoicing in Christ in spite of his rough treatment in chains? I wonder how many were converted by his unwavering devotion and consistency to Christ during those two years? The Lord was his strength, and the gospel was taken by those who did believe outside the palace walls and Paul's hired house all over the city of Rome. From Philippians 1:13 and 4:22, we find that many royal soldiers and chief men were won to Christ by Paul. In the years to follow one of the early church fathers, Tertullian, would write that the Roman government was disturbed when it was discovered that there were Christians in positions of authority.

Sometimes our best witness is given through a good attitude when we are most afflicted. Evangelist Craig Bryan was a pastor in Michigan for many years. His wife took ill with a cancer that eventually took her life, but before she died, she and her husband led 120 doctors, nurses and medical professionals to Christ. She had a sweet spirit and a bore the fruits of righteousness in her affliction.

Paul had preached Christ to all kinds of people in all kinds of places. *Acts 9:15 But the Lord said unto him, Go thy way: for he is a chosen vessel unto me, to bear my name before the Gentiles, and kings, and the children of Israel...*God had told Paul that he would preach to gentiles, kings and Israel. Paul had preached all over Israel, Asia and now Europe. He had preached to the religious but lost, the common people and the procurial governors of Israel, but now he was before Caesar himself. Paul had always wanted to preach in Rome. He had already written his epistle to the saints there about four years before arriving in Rome himself. Now his dream was coming true, just not the way he thought it would. There is a touch of divine irony here. Paul came to Rome as a prisoner not a preacher. As a preacher, he would have paid his own way. As a prisoner, Rome footed the bill for Paul's passage, protection and housing so that Paul could preach in Caesar's own house.

There were those who before were not bold to preach Christ. They had Paul to preach for them. As long as Paul was preaching, they felt no compulsion to do poorly what Paul could do clearly. Now that Paul was in prison, his converts had to become bold and begin to do for themselves those things that Paul had done for them in the past. His chains stirred his preacher boys to action and gave them great boldness in the gospel. We find this also happened with Peter and John in the book of Acts. *Acts 4:13 Now when they saw the boldness of Peter and John, and perceived that they were unlearned and ignorant men, they marvelled; and they took knowledge of them, that they had been with Jesus.* Then we are told later in the chapter: *Acts 4:31 And when they had prayed, the place was shaken where they were assembled together; and they were all filled with the Holy Ghost, and they spake the word of God with boldness.* These men drew their boldness from the boldness of Peter and John.

Some folks say, "I wish I could witness for God like they do, but I am not as good at it as they are." We were all lousy at one time. Be bold and God will strengthen you. *Ephesians 6:10 Finally, my brethren, be strong in the Lord, and in the power of his might.* Christ will help you with your words if you will be bold in your walk and witness.

Even though this is the book of rejoicing, Paul mentions envy and strife on numerous occasions in this epistle. As great a church as Philippi was, there was strife and envy at Philippi. The word "strife" means "to stir up." It seems there is always someone who is trying to stir something up in the church. Many try to avoid strife by avoiding church. There is no avoiding strife in this life no matter where you go. Paul warns against envy and strife in all four chapters and even mentions two women by name. There is no one who is exempt from unpleasant divisions in life. Paul rejoiced and pressed on in spite of them.

There were those who were stirred to preach Christ boldly when Paul was imprisoned. There were others who took advantage of Paul's imprisonment by belittling Paul and his preaching. They were cowards when Paul was out preaching, but now that he was bound they had found their false courage. Paul was not present to rebuke them or give a fair defense for himself. These men were false proponents of the gospel who were secretly pleased that Paul was in prison. Now they could steal the affections of the saints and try to win them to themselves whereas Paul was simply trying to win them to Christ. It is good counsel to never follow a man who is a surprise critic pretending to be a preacher. These men were not preaching Christ and His gospel in a sincere and pure manner. They added a broken heart to the chains that were already keeping Paul bound. Paul rejoiced in spite of both afflictions and bonds.

It has been said that the gospel needs no defence. That is not necessarily true. Paul defended the truth by upholding the truth and contending against all the lies propagated amongst the gospel. Jude tells us to earnestly contend for our faith. The gospel is often misrepresented. The Judaizers demanded the works of men in addition to the work of Christ in Paul's day. Two thousand years later nothing has changed. Men today still misrepresent the gospel in this same way. Salvation is Jesus Christ plus nothing and minus nothing. It is through Christ and Christ alone. It is our duty to make sure the gospel is represented correctly.

Paul rejoiced that Christ was being preached. Christ was being preached in pretence. This refers to those who preached Christ in hope of some personal gain for themselves, which is very un-Christ like. The word "pretence" here means that they preached for pay or in order to make a living. They wanted to develop a career and make a life for themselves. They had the right message, but they lacked the proper motivation. However, Christ was also being preached in truth. The simple clarity and purity of the life and gospel of Jesus for the gain of heaven and not for the sake of men. These men realized that they are only instruments of God's will for God's glory. As long as Christ was preached, Paul did not care who received credit, and he could even put up with those who had the right message even if they did not have the right motive. At least the controversy was over Christ and not Apollo or Mercury. If Christ was being preached, the truth would eventually come forth.

Paul's Purpose- Philippians 1:19-26

Philippians 1:19-26 *For I know that this shall turn to my salvation through your prayer, and the supply of the Spirit of Jesus Christ, According to my earnest expectation and my hope, that in nothing I shall be ashamed, but that with all boldness, as always, so now also Christ shall be magnified in my body, whether it be by life, or by death. For to me to live is Christ, and to die is gain. But if I live in the flesh, this is the fruit of my labour: yet what I shall choose I wot not. For I am in a strait betwixt two, having a desire to depart, and to be with Christ; which is far better: Nevertheless to abide in the flesh is more needful for you. And having this confidence, I know that I shall abide and continue with you all for your furtherance and joy of faith; That your rejoicing may be more abundant in Jesus Christ for me by my coming to you again.*

These verses show us how much Paul depended on the prayers of the people. Sometimes we look at someone like a Paul and think that they can help us but we are of no help to them. Paul needed the church to know that as much as he helped them, he also needed their help. Paul realized that neither he nor the church could do anything without the help of God. Paul never thought himself so well off spiritually or so important that he was without the need of the prayers of the church. We can never overestimate the value and the need for prayer. It is worthy to note that in nearly every epistle Paul pleaded for the saints to pray for him; however, Paul never asked for the prayers of the saints until after he had first prayed for them. Paul prayed for others before he asked for prayer for himself. It is a sad prayer life indeed that asks for prayer from others but does not pray for others first. I believe heaven dulls its ears to the prayers of those who ask for prayer but do not pray themselves. We cannot expect God to move on behalf of the prayers of others while we ourselves are living prayerless lives.

Paul was as saved as he was ever going to be, but the prayers of the saints might be his deliverance from Roman bonds to preach the gospel once again before he died. Remember also that there were two groups preaching the gospel in Rome. One group preached Christ sincerely and purely, but the Judaizers preached Christ in pretense. The Judaizers taught that an individual must pass through the ceremonies of the Old Covenant to come to Christ in the New. Even though the Judaizers preached Christ to their own advantage, some truth was being given and if the truth was made known, those innocents who had been lied to might find their way to the truth. I have met countless Christians who attended a church with poor doctrine and an impure gospel but they got enough truth to be truly saved or put them on the right track to salvation. Eventually, God leads one with a sincere heart to a church where they will find a sincere gospel- Jesus without wax as we mentioned earlier.

When God is real to us, and we receive all things either by His permission or appointment, we can find occasions for joy where other men see unmitigated grief, chinks of blue in the dark sky, and songs in the night. ~F.B. Meyer

Whatever Paul's present conditions were, his prospect was always the same. Whether Paul was free or imprisoned, he expected Christ to be manifested in his life to whoever he was brought into contact with. Paul never focused on circumstances. He always focused on his objective. His objective was to make Christ known by magnifying and glorifying Christ in his mortal body. Paul could do that at any time and in any place. Many Christians are defeated by their present circumstances. They are defeated because they lose sight of their objective. I have seen Christians going through what we would consider to be positive circumstances, but they were defeated in spirit. They either lost sight of their objective or have allowed another objective, different from Christ, to take a preeminent place. Paul's objective was always the same- Christ magnified and glorified. When

Paul awoke in the morning, chained to a Roman praetorian, his thoughts and ambitions for the day were not how could he be freed from his bonds. He immediately turned to promoting the glory of his Savior.

Paul asked the church to pray for the supply of the Spirit of Jesus Christ. The Holy Spirit is the Spirit of Christ. In other epistles Paul speaks of the Holy Spirit as "the Spirit of Jesus Christ," "the Spirit of the Son," "the Spirit of life in Christ Jesus," and "as the Spirit of Jesus." Consider these facts about Christ and the Holy Spirit:

- ✢ Jesus was conceived by the Holy Ghost- Matthew 1:20.
- ✢ Jesus was anointed by the Holy Ghost at His baptism- Matthew 3:16.
- ✢ Jesus was filled with the Holy Ghost when He was led into the wilderness to be tempted- Luke 4:1, 14.
- ✢ Jesus wrought His miracles and spoke His words in the power of the Holy Ghost- Acts 2:22.
- ✢ Jesus yielded Himself to His Father in death by the power of the Holy Ghost- Luke 23:46.
- ✢ Jesus was raised from the dead by the power of the Holy Ghost- Romans 8:11.
- ✢ Acts 1:2 tells us that during the forty days after His resurrection and before His ascension Jesus...*through the Holy Ghost had given commandments unto the apostles whom he had chosen.*

The word supply is used in the sense of receiving that which is necessary to meet a need or reach an objective. Paul would never be able to magnify Christ in his life without the supply of the Holy Spirit of Christ. The Holy Spirit has a ministry of supply to the saints. His supply is sufficient and inexhaustible for all believers. The Holy Spirit supplies certain things to us:

† Comfort- John 14:26.

† Counsel- John 14:26; 1 Corinthians 2:9-10.

† Courage- John 15:26-27.

† Conviction- John 16:7.

Then there are things that He supplies on our behalf:

† He Saves us by regeneration- Titus 3:5.

† He Supplicates for us in prayer- Romans 8:26.

† He Strengthens our inner man- Ephesians 3:16.

The Greek word of expectation is *apokaradokia*. *Apo* means "away from", *kara* means "head", *dokein* means "to look." Simply defined, the word expectation means to look away from everything but the head or that which is most important- the object of our desire. It carries the thought of "lifting up our head." *Luke 21:28 And when these things begin to come to pass, then look up, and lift up your heads; for your redemption draweth nigh.* It also implies as when one stands on the tips of their toes to peer over a fence. Paul speaks in Romans about our expectation of the resurrection when the day shall reveal the glorification of the sons of God. *Romans 8:19 For the earnest expectation of the creature waiteth for the manifestation of the sons of God.* What is your expectation of life? We could also ask this question in other ways. What do you expect to get out of life? What is most important in your life? What captivates your inner most thoughts? What is it that occupies your mind whenever your mind has a chance to wander for a few moments? What gets the attention of your heart? What drives you? What are your ambitions? The truth is that a great many Christians if not most live very selfishly. We spend most of our life and labor striving for things that satisfy the desires of the natural man. Very few are completely sold out to the Lord Jesus Christ in such a way that all of their life and death itself has only Christ and eternity on their mind. We live in a materialistic world that grasps for whatever it can get, whenever it can get it, by whatever means necessary. The world is in desperate need of Christians who are sold out, selfless and sacrificial. Paul was certainly this kind of Christian. He gives us a model and a method to pursue.

Paul's expectation and hope were his forward look towards Christ...*that in nothing I shall be ashamed.* Paul did not want to be ashamed in any area of his life when he gave an account to Christ. About four years before Paul was imprisoned he wrote to the church of Corinth in *2 Corinthians 5:10 For we must all appear before the judgment seat of Christ; that every one may receive the things done in his body, according to that he hath done, whether it be good or bad.* The word "appear" means "to manifest without disguise." Who we really are and what we truly lived for will be revealed in the day of judgment. Many profess Christ is all, but judgment will reveal the truth. In the preceding verse, Paul said that he wanted to be...*accepted of him*...Paul was already accepted *in* Christ. He wanted to be accepted *of* Christ. The apostle John tells us that if we have demonstrated perfect love for Christ by obedience to His commands we may have boldness in the day of our judgment. *1 John 4:17 Herein is our love made perfect, that we may have boldness in the day of judgment: because as he is, so are we in this world.* Where there is boldness, there is no shame. Paul knew that if he magnified Christ in his body, whether in life or by death, he would have boldness in the day of judgment. Paul was not magnifying his body. He was magnifying Christ in his body. Christ is bodily in heaven, but He still desires that His life be made manifest to the world. Christ is so distant from this world today. Someone once gave the analogy that the body of a Christian is like a telescope that brings the sinner a sense of the nearness of Christ. Christ uses our bodies as His instrument to make Himself known. This is part of the work of our redemption. *1 Corinthians 6:19-20 What? know ye not that your body is the temple of the Holy Ghost which is in you, which ye have of God, and ye are not your own? For ye are bought with a price: therefore glorify God in your body, and in your spirit, which are God's.* Our bodies belong to God. God wants us to sacrifice our bodies to Him for Christ's use. That is what Paul told the church at

Rome. *Romans 12:1 I beseech you therefore, brethren, by the mercies of God, that ye present your bodies a living sacrifice, holy, acceptable unto God, which is your reasonable service.* God owns our bodies. He wants to use our bodies to bring glory to Him and the knowledge of His Son to those who are blinded by Satan. Christian, have you ever dedicated your body to God? Have you consecrated your life's work for His work? God has ordained your body for His glory and to make Christ known. What are you doing with it? Do you spend all your effort in glorifying your body or glorifying Christ?

Four young men- Daniel, Hananiah, Azariah, and Mishael- dedicated their bodies in order to magnify God. They refused the king's meat and wine- Daniel 1:8. They refused to defile their bodies by disobeying God in order to please an earthly king. They magnified God in their bodies and God protected them. Later, three of those young men refused to bow their bodies to the image of gold. Again, God protected their bodies in the fiery furnace and Nebuchadnezzar again magnified God. King Nebuchadnezzar magnified God because of their obedience. *Daniel 3:28 Then Nebuchadnezzar spake, and said, Blessed be the God of Shadrach, Meshach, and Abednego, who hath sent his angel, and delivered his servants that trusted in him, and have changed the king's word, and yielded their bodies, that they might not serve nor worship any god, except their own God.* In order for God to be magnified, God must be made manifest. In order for God to be magnified, someone has to take a public stand for right and bear the reproach of the world.

We see how God was magnified through the life of Daniel and his companions, but often God has been magnified through the death of his saints. John the Baptist and Paul were both beheaded. Peter was crucified. *Foxe's Book of Martyrs* tells us of countless who magnified Christ through their death. Polycarp, James the Just, Albas (the first martyr of England), John Wycliffe, John Huss, William Tyndale, Lady Jane Grey, Latimer, Ridley and all rest of the saints that passed through the fires of Smithfield, England magnified Christ by their life but are remembered for how they magnified Christ in their deaths. We know little of the lives of the martyr's. We know them by their death. Their death magnified Christ. It will be sad indeed for those who follow this crowd at the Bema Seat of Christ after having traded eternal treasures for earthly toys all their life.

While many Christians are troubled in a troubled world, Paul was only concerned with the magnification of Christ whether in life or death. Paul went the limit for his Lord. For Paul, Christ was the only real reason for living and dying. It grieves me to hear a professing child of God claim that they have nothing to live for. If you have Christ you have everything to live for. If you have Christ you have everything to die for. Christ was also magnified by His own life and death. His life and death has caused more controversy than any other life in the history of the world. His life and death brought salvation to all who would receive it. Should not the life and death of Christ continue its work in our bodies in both life and death today?

If you were to take away the words "Christ" and "gain" you would see how closely related life and death are. They would be separated only by a punctuation mark. I have often heard pastors illustrate the relationship of life and death through the analogy of a tombstone. On a tombstone there is the date of the day you are born and the date of the day you died. The only thing that connects those dates is a symbol called a dash. Your life- all that lies between the beginning and the end of your life- is just a dash. Our lives are truly a vapor that appear for a time and then vanish away. Life is a portal to death. Death is the portal to eternity.

Dr. William Pettingill was a contemporary of R.A. Torrey. The two even wrote a book together. Dr. Pettingill used to say that gain is more of the same thing. If Paul died, he would only have more of Jesus than he ever had before. To die was to gain more of Christ. Paul was resolved and at perfect peace with all that was before him. If Paul continued to live, he would continue to bear the fruits of righteousness as Christ did. He wins Christ by winning others to Christ. If he dies, he is with Christ. To be absent from the body is to be present with the Lord. Certainly that is personal gain. Either way he has Christ. To live is to gain Christ. To die is personal gain. To live is to make Christ known. To die is to know Christ like we have never known Him before- to be with Him bodily for eternity. Death is not an enemy to the child of God who truly claims Christ as all. The Old Testament tells us in Ecclesiastes that ...*Precious in the eyes of the Lord is the death of his saints.* Our death is precious to God because we will be eternally with God. Paul was saying that death was not only precious to God, but it was precious to himself to be with God.

My body will be the theatre in which Christ's glory is displayed.
~Unknown

The glory of Christ ought to be the end of our life, the grace of Christ the principle of our life, and the word of Christ the rule of it.
~Matthew Henry

Sadly, not every child of God carries Paul's desire. Many would say, "For me to live is money." "For me to live is self." "For me to live is fame." "For me to live is worldly pleasure." "For me to live is to do as little as possible." "For me to live is position or power or both." "For me to live is career." "For me to live is family." "For me to live is financial security." "For me to live is athletics." "For me to live is to glorify my body." "For me to live is materialism."

For the child of God, death is a final and complete union with Christ and reunion with the saints. It is eternal communion with both. Those who live for Christ will come to realize that death is gain. Death is not a misfortune or the end of all things, nor something to be feared. Death only brings you closer to Christ. Death is more of Christ not less. Paul looked at death as a departure. He also used this term when writing to Timothy. *2 Timothy 4:6 For I am now ready to be offered, and the time of my departure is at hand.* In Paul's day a departure carried the idea of a ship loosing its moorings to set sail for a journey. Paul would leave this earth and find himself on heaven's bright shore. This world was never Paul's home. Paul related to Abraham as he penned the book of Hebrews. *Hebrews 11:9-10, 13 By faith he sojourned in the land of promise, as in a strange country, dwelling in tabernacles with Isaac and Jacob, the heirs with him of the same promise: For he looked for a city which hath foundations, whose builder and maker is God. These all died in faith, not having received the promises, but having seen them afar off, and were persuaded of them, and embraced them, and confessed that they were strangers and pilgrims on the earth.* The problem with many Christians is that they have made this world their home and heaven is a foreign land to them. Many Christians are settlers and not pilgrims. A pilgrim is a foreigner and a traveler who is just passing through. A settler puts down his roots and stays. Abraham was a pilgrim. Lot was a settler. The results of Abraham's faith and Lot's foolishness are made clear to us through their lives.

Christian, we are citizens of heaven. *Ephesians 2:19 Now therefore ye are no more strangers and foreigners, but fellowcitizens with the saints, and of the household of God... Philippians 3:20 For our conversation is in heaven; from whence also we look for the Saviour, the Lord Jesus Christ...*The word "conversation" that Paul uses in Philippians comes from the root of the same word he uses for "citizens" in Ephesians. These verses teach us to bear the identity and the conduct of heavenly citizens.

Paul said that he was in a great strait between his desire to continue to bear fruit on earth for Christ and to be with Christ eternally. The word he uses for a great strait is *senechomai.* The Greeks would use this word for a traveler in a narrow passage with a wall of rock on either side. Today we would say that Paul was between a rock and a hard place. To magnify Christ in his body on the earth was a great work and privilege. To depart and be with Christ eternally would be the culmination of his heart's greatest desire.

To live on earth is to continue to bear fruit in the body of Christ. We cannot bear fruit in heaven. All opportunities to serve and make an eternal difference in the lives of the lost are given only on earth. As long as Paul was on the earth, he could suffer for Christ as Christ suffered for him. F.B. Meyer gave a short list reflecting this text on Christ our life:

- † Christ is the origin of our life.
- † Christ must be the essence of our life.
- † Christ must also be the model of our life.
- † Christ is to be the aim of our life.
- † Christ is the solace of our life.
- † Christ is the reward of our life.

Happy must be the Christian whose heart truly claims the life of Christ for their own.

Most folks have a natural aversion or fear of death. For the world, death is the end of all things. For the saint of God, death is the beginning of all things that will never end. Most saints look at death apprehensively at best. Paul was one of those rare saints who lived so close to Christ that he truly longed for death. Death for the child of God is another birth. The Bible tells us that Jesus is the first begotten from the dead. Those who have part in the resurrection will experience the fullness of the new birth by their entrance into everlasting life. The Greek language uses several different tenses. Every word in the New Testament referring to salvation uses the "aorist" tense. The aorist tense in the Greek always signifies eternal, everlasting, something done that can never be undone. Salvation is the promise of everlasting life that can never be undone. Paul had seen Christ in the third heavens, and he had suffered physically on the earth. He had experienced great physical pain on several occasions. He was beaten with rods three times. He was stoned and left for dead. He was shipwrecked and in the deep a day and a night. Paul was not afraid of the physical sting of death. Paul knew the physical pain of death would be his last suffering. He knew that it would release him to the presence of his Savior. Only then would he be free from all the pains and cares of this world. Paul loved his Lord so much, and so longed to see Jesus, that he longed for death. A Christian who lives for Jesus on the earth longs to see through the veil and look on Christ. Death is our veil. We pass through the veil of the valley of the shadow of death to be bodily with Christ for all eternity. Paul told the church in Corinth that now we see through a glass darkly. In his day that would be a highly polished piece of brass that would cast a reflection. Today we might better relate it to a piece of tinted glass or a two way mirror. We know Christ is on the other side, but we cannot see Him as clearly as we would like to. John also spoke of this veil that hides Christ from us. *1 John 3:2 Beloved, now are we the sons of God, and it doth not yet appear what we shall be: but we know that, when he shall appear, we shall be like him; for we shall see him as he is.*

Paul was in a strait. He was caught between two things that he loved dearly. He loved serving Christ in this world, and yet he longed to enjoy the presence of Christ in heaven. Life was rich, full and sweet because Christ's life was Paul's life. Death was sweet because it brought him into the fullness of Christ. Both were sweet to Paul, and he did not know how to choose between the two. It was not for Paul to decide between the two. If Christ left him on earth, he would bear fruit and glorify Christ. If Christ called him home, he would gladly go. Those who long for heaven must be willing to labor for Christ in this world as long as God has a work for them to do. It often seems that these are the ones that God leaves here the longest. Those who love God more, labor more abundantly for God. We are here because Christ needs us here now more than we need to be with Him.

Serve out your enlistment. When a soldier is nearing the end of his enlistment, he often gets what is called "short timer's disease." When you know your time is short and your tour of duty is almost done, it is easy to get lazy and careless. Many a life has been lost in battle or at the least the rest of the team has suffered, because of the neglect of a short timer. Don't get short timer's disease. Paul was not looking for an escape from the work of Christ. It has been well said that Christians might be weary in the work, but we are never to be weary of the work. He simply desired more of Christ. More could only be found by entering into the eternal presence of Christ. The best part of heaven is not being reunited with family and friends. It is not streets of gold, gates of pearl or walls of jasper clear as crystal. The best part of heaven is not the river of life or the tree of life. The best part of heaven is to be bodily with Jesus for all eternity. Paul could be with Jesus in spirit. His soul was sealed by the Spirit of promise until the day of redemption, yet he longed for more. He desired the bodily presence of Christ.

Paul uses the word "confidence" more than twenty times in the Scripture. He uses it more than any other New Testament writer. Paul did not live apprehensively or with a fear of the unknown. He lived with confidence and boldness. Paul was confident that he and the church at Philippi would continue in the furtherance of the gospel in faith and joy. The only real joy for a Christian is to continue beyond the faith that saves them and walk in the life of faith that sustains them.

Paul hoped to see the Philippians again. He knew that the church at Philippi would rejoice in Jesus if they were able to see him one more time. From what we can tell from church history, it appears that Paul was freed for a short period of time before being imprisoned again and sentenced to death. I am sure, from what we have already learned of Paul's close relationship to this good church, that if it was at all possible he returned to Philippi one last time. There are certain Christians that when I see them I rejoice. There are others that when I meet them, they are a source of weariness, contention or bad news. We would all do well to live in such a way as to bring a rejoicing spirit when we come into the presence of others Christians. All rejoicing for God's people should begin and end with Christ. That rejoicing should increase unto an abundance that overflows our heart.

Paul's Plea- Philippians 1:27-30

Philippians 1:27-30 *Only let your conversation be as it becometh the gospel of Christ: that whether I come and see you, or else be absent, I may hear of your affairs, that ye stand fast in one spirit, with one mind striving together for the faith of the gospel; And in nothing terrified by your adversaries: which is to them an evident token of perdition, but to you of salvation, and that of God. For unto you it is given in the behalf of Christ, not only to believe on him, but also to suffer for his sake; Having the same conflict which ye saw in me, and now hear to be in me.*

Up until this point, Paul has been speaking to the Philippians in the first person. He has been more or less autobiographical, with the exception of his prayer in verses nine through eleven. Now he shifts his message for the remainder of his epistle. He wants to apply these spiritual truths for the saints of Philippi. Paul was not one, like many today, to speak in broad generalities without bringing his message to a point of personal application. All teaching and preaching that is without personal application is vain. It is nice to hear, but it has no value and adds no strength to the believer. Truth must be applied. Here in these final four verses of chapter one Paul makes a plea. He pleads for the saints at Philippi to do three things:

- † Paul pleas for them to *stand* together.
- † Paul pleas for them to *strive* together.
- † Paul pleas for them to *suffer* together.

The word conversation here is the Greek word *politeuo*. We derive our words "politics" and "police" from this word. Our conversation is how we conduct ourselves. It means "to exercise our citizenship." Paul was writing from Rome itself. Paul had Roman citizenship. That is what brought him to trial in Rome. Remember that Philippi was a Roman colony. Roman colonies were small parts of Rome planted throughout the known world where Roman citizens never forgot they were Romans. No matter how far they were from Rome, Rome was with them because Rome was woven into their hearts. They knew the privileges and responsibilities of their Roman citizenship. We are citizens of heaven. Should a child of God do any less than a child of the devil? Should a heavenly citizen do less than an earthly citizen. We are to live like heavenly citizens on the earth just as Abraham did. We are to take Heaven with us everywhere we go. We should wear its righteous garments. We should speak its Biblical language. We should use heavenly titles such as Brother, Sister, Saint, Deacon and Pastor.

Our Eternal Father writes to us from our capital city- the New Jerusalem- reminding our earthly colonies, that we call churches, to remember whose we are and what we are. A Christian's conduct ought to be a credit to the gospel of the Christ Who lived and died to save them.

Paul illustrates our conversation through the use of the word "becometh." This simply means appropriate. Our conversation is to become us or be appropriate. This is certainly contrary to those who teach that since they are under grace, all things are lawful. All things are lawful but not all things are expedient- appropriate for the Christian. The word becometh is a word used to compliment someone who is able to appropriately match their physical features with their garments. Not everything looks good on everyone. Many ladies will identify their complexion by saying that they are a fall, winter, spring or summer. This tells them what colors will make them look "becoming", whereas another season will not compliment them. You might hear someone say that a particular dress is becoming on a lady or that a particular suit is becoming on a man. They are saying that the garments enhance the face and the features of the one wearing them. Paul said it this way to Titus in *Titus 2:10 Not purloining, but shewing all good fidelity; that they may adorn the doctrine of God our Saviour in all things.* Does your religion become you? Do the garments and the doctrines of Christ and His righteousness adorn you? What do you invest in time, effort and money for your spiritual life, as opposed to what you invest in your physical body?

Paul desired to come and see the Philippians once again before he died. Once more, Paul desired to sail to the coast of Neapolis to be met by dear friends and elders, who would take him back to the church that bears this colony's name. We are not totally certain that it ever happened. Paul was not certain that it ever would happen. So he admonishes his beloved in the Lord, that whether he is able to come and see them or whether he remains absent...*Let your conversation be as it becometh the gospel of Christ.* Paul was going to hear of their affairs. What was he going to hear? Heaven will hear of our affairs. There is an accuser of the brethren (Satan) who stands day and night before the throne of God telling all the evil he sees and none of the good.

Paul tells us to stand fast. This is a military order. It is an order to hold the line against an overwhelming enemy. There have been more than a few soldiers who have looked forward to going to battle for the very first time. They have usually trained for one to two years. They have seen their bodies pushed physically beyond what they have thought possible. They have been mentally pushed beyond what they have thought humanly possible. They have become experts in weaponry to the point where they fear no one. They cannot wait until their very first battle. They desire to see all their training and ability proven. They stand in the morning light. But who will still be standing when the night falls? Who will still be standing when the battle is not won as quickly and as easily as they thought it would be? Even among the most elite of our soldiers and battle hardened veterans, there have been those who ceased to stand in the face of an overwhelming enemy. Many have turned and run. Someone has to stand. We live in the days of apostasy. Men are departing from the life of faith, and though they have the promise of eternal life in heaven, they are dying spiritually on the earth.

The only way to stand against the overwhelming enemy is to strive together. It has been said that we must all stand together, or we all die separately. That is exactly what Paul is pleading for here. In the Old Testament we have stories of battle, where in the midst of overwhelming foes and confusion, whole armies turned against each other and destroyed themselves. Nothing can hurt the testimony of Christ and His church as much as a church at strife. The church should strive together and not be at strife against each other. Strife always comes from the individual pride and the self-will of the people. If Satan can disrupt the ranks of the church, he wins for himself a great victory. The house of God must stand united or it will fall. Our Captain told us so while He walked the earth. *Matthew 12:25 And Jesus knew their thoughts, and said unto them, Every kingdom divided against itself is brought to desolation; and every city or house divided against itself shall not stand...* Let the world have the strife and quarreling. Let the church strive together not against each other.

We must stand and strive with one mind. We have a common cause and a common goal that is greater than ourselves. We have our orders from heaven. We have been given the command called the Great Commission. It is time for the church to move together and strive together for the faith. The gospel is greater than our lives. It is worth more than we are. We are unified through Christ and receive our orders through His Word. Though we may have differences among ourselves, our differences are not worth anything when they are compared to the goal of reaching a lost world. I am speaking of petty differences and preferences, not immutable Bible doctrine. There is no compromise on truth.

If religion is worth anything, it is worth everything. ~Matthew Henry

Paul was chained to a Roman Praetorian, yet he pleaded boldly for the church not to be terrified by their adversaries. A Christian that is terrified demonstrates a weakness to the enemy. The enemy will smell their fear and go after the weak link. To them, our terror is a token of perdition- being lost and destroyed. The truth is, no matter what an enemy does to a Christian, we have salvation from God. We may be delivered from our present sufferings in this life or perhaps be received into everlasting life. It is a great truth, and a great comfort, for the child of God to realize and accept that the end of all suffering is to be saved by our God.

Faith and suffering for Christ are inseparable experiences of the Christian life. Where there is one, there will be the other. Every person who identifies with Christ in salvation will suffer with Christ as well. *John 15:20 Remember the word that I said unto you, The servant is not greater than his lord. If they have persecuted me, they will also persecute you; if they have kept my saying, they will keep yours also. 2 Timothy 3:12 Yea, and all that will live godly in Christ Jesus shall suffer persecution.* Most Christians look on suffering as a punishment or some type of judgment from God. The truth is that suffering is a gift that comes with our salvation. Our suffering is precious to God. Many Christians feel that they have "arrived" spiritually, because they have lived their lives in moderation, and have acquired victory over some sins and besetting sin. The truth is that we have only "arrived" when we suffer. Suffering is what will take you to some point of glory for Christ in your life. Victory over sin is a natural growth process. Suffering is the destination that will bring God glory through your life. Suffering is the high calling of God in Christ Jesus.

Paul reminded the Philippians that the suffering they had seen and now heard of in his life, would be a part of their lives as well. Our lives will be filled with conflict. The word conflict means "a struggle for a prize." Yes there is suffering and conflict, but there is also a prize. Paul speaks of it in the next chapter. *Philippians 3:13-14 Brethren, I count not myself to have apprehended: but this one thing I do, forgetting those things which are behind, and reaching forth unto those things which are before, I press toward the mark for the prize of the high calling of God in Christ Jesus.* Paul tells us in *2 Timothy 2:12 If we suffer, we shall also reign with him: if we deny him, he also will deny us...*Remember the words of the English martyr Hugh Latimer to his friend Nicholas Ridley? *"Be of good comfort, Master Ridley and play the man, we shall this day light such a candle, by God's grace, in*

81

England, as I trust shall never be put out." Their martyrdom in the fires of Smithfield still encourages us today. Remember there is a prize for our conflicts and sufferings. We shall be eternally with Christ ruling and reigning in His eternal kingdom.

Chapter 2

Rejoicing In Christ Our Paradigm

Chapter two continues in the personal and practical application that Paul began to impart at the close of chapter one. Paul does not stop pleading at the close of chapter one. He continues to plead in chapter two. We know this because chapter two begins with the word "therefore." In light of Paul's plea, he continues to expand his plea by challenging believers to follow a paradigm (pattern or example) that will bring rejoicing to the church. Of course this paradigm is the earthly life of Christ. Paul is not speaking about imitation but impartation. There is a difference. Imitation is to copy. Impartation is to receive a gift. Imitators of Christ are typically false Christ's or anti-Christ's. They are not the real thing. Things that are different are not the same.

There is a difference between butter and margarine. It has been claimed that margarine is more "heart healthy." In fact, margarine is only one molecule off from being plastic. It raises LDL cholesterol (the bad cholesterol) and lowers HDL cholesterol (the good one). Margarine lowers your immune system and increases risks of cancer.

It is an imitation. Butter actually has vitamins and minerals that are not found in margarine. An imitation is not the real thing and causes harm under the pretense that it is better. Impartation is to be given the real thing. When I received Christ as my Savior, He took my death and gave me His life. He imparted His life to me *Titus 3:5b-6...by the washing of regeneration, and renewing of the Holy Ghost; Which he shed on us abundantly through Jesus Christ our Saviour.* A new birth imparts a new life. *2 Corinthians 5:17 Therefore if any man be in Christ, he is a new creature: old things are passed away; behold, all things are become new.*

Christ has left us an example that we should follow in His steps. He has imparted His Spirit into our lives to guide us. Of course the flesh is still present, so we must choose to follow what is right. God never forces His will on man. He does not force us into salvation. God takes no one hostage to heaven. He does not force us into sanctification, but God does give us all we need to fulfill His will. He imparts to us an example to follow and places a guide, called the Holy Spirit, within us. In this chapter Paul will teach us to rejoice in the paradigm of Christ that has been imparted to us in four different ways. Paul will also reveal to us in this chapter the seven steps down to Christ's humility and the seven steps up to Christ's exaltation.

Rejoice In Christ's Paradigm Of Mind- Philippians 2:1-8
Philippians 2:1-8 *If there be therefore any consolation in Christ, if any comfort of love, if any fellowship of the Spirit, if any bowels and*

mercies, Fulfil ye my joy, that ye be likeminded, having the same love, being of one accord, of one mind. Let nothing be done through strife or vainglory; but in lowliness of mind let each esteem other better than themselves. Look not every man on his own things, but every man also on the things of others. Let this mind be in you, which was also in Christ Jesus: Who, being in the form of God, thought it not robbery to be equal with God: But made himself of no reputation, and took upon him the form of a servant, and was made in the likeness of men: And being found in fashion as a man, he humbled himself, and became obedient unto death, even the death of the cross.

In verses one through four we are shown the mind that Christ desires for us to have. In verses five through eight we are shown how Christ Himself set us an example while He lived on the earth. The last word of verse four is the key word for all eight verses. It is the word "others." Others is to be the sum of the mind of the Christian, as it was in the mind of Christ. Living for others is the key connection between humility and honor.

Paul begins this chapter with the word "if" in relation to consolation in Christ, the fellowship of the Spirit and bowels of mercy. The word "if" is not a conditional suggestion in this context. The apostle Paul often used the word "if" as an argument, as opposed to a condition. Paul taught and thought logically. It has been said of Paul's epistles that if you are not reading logically, you are not reading Paul. There is certainly consolation in Christ. In 2 Corinthians 1, Paul tells the church at Corinth about the consolation of Christ in great detail. There is comfort of love. We are taught about our great Comforter in John 14-16. The Bible also teaches us the certainty of the fellowship of the Spirit. John 14,16, & 17 and 1 Corinthians 2 explain this to us in great detail. 2 Corinthians 13:14 tells us of the communion of the Holy Ghost. The word communion is the very same Greek word used here for fellowship. We have inward fellowship with God. There are bowels of mercy. In Isaiah 63 and Jeremiah 31 God tells us of His bowels of mercy for Israel. Paul told the church of Colosse to put on bowels of mercies.

You could also use the phrases "since there is" or "in view of the fact" in place of the word "if." Paul is saying that if (since, in view of the fact) you have experienced the consolation of Christ, the comfort of God's love, the fellowship of God's Spirit and the mercies of God, then love each other in the same way that God expresses His love to you. Christians ought to console and comfort each other. They ought to love each other and enjoy fellowship with each other. We ought to be merciful to each other as God is merciful to us- Ephesians 4:32. These gifts from above are incentives for Christians to live together in peace and strive together in the work of Christ and His gospel.

Paul goes on to say, in light of all these things that were imparted to you when I came and gave you the gospel, fulfill my joy. Paul loved everyone in Philippi. He had begotten them in the Lord. He wanted to see them all love each other as he loved each of them. This would bring Paul more joy. This would make Paul's joy full. Paul's joy was fulfilled with church unity because God's joy is fulfilled in the same way. Our heavenly Father loves to see His family get along. He expects us to be one in love, accord, and mind. There was good reason for the Holy Spirit to inspire Paul to exhort the church to be like-minded, with the same love, accord and mind. The law of the flesh is resistant to all four of these divine impartations. The one thing that threatened the church at Philippi was disunity. In chapter four Paul will name those who were bringing disunity into the church. It is human nature to express or own thoughts, love only who and what we want as we wish and to expect all people to be in accord with our will and to come around to our way of thinking. Many churches are in a mess simply because this one verse is not being practically applied within the local autonomous body of Christ. There is no rejoicing in Christ within a church that is in such a state.

You can put men together for a time and a common cause will bind them together. Paul was reminding them that the church has a common cause and devotion. We are to be devoted to the person of Jesus Christ Who loved us and died to save us. We are to advance His gospel through the membership of His body- the Church. Our cause and our devotion will never compromise in matters of doctrine, but it does allows us to lay aside petty differences and opinions. Our cultural, economic, social and ethnic differences should all be laid aside, and we are to come together through Jesus Christ for His coming kingdom and present and eternal glory.

There is to be the same love for all men in the church. The word love here is the Greek word *agape*. This is God's greatest love. It is the deep abiding love of God for all mankind. It is a love that loves not just in word but in deed and in truth- 1 John 3:18. It is both a giving and a selfless love. Paul told the church at Rome to let their love be without dissimulation. That means we are not to pick and choose who we love. God loved the world and gave His Son for all. We are to have the same love for all men. If Christians would love Christians like Jesus loved His enemies, we would have revival in our churches. Christians should have a love that cannot be conquered by our prejudices our differences or our enemies. Our love is to be greater than that. It should be greater than the hate that is shown to us by our enemies. We do not just love the ones that love us. We love the unlovely, and those who hate us.

We are to be of one accord. A musical chord is made up of three notes. For example the notes in the C chord are C, E and G. If you play an A in the chord, you will have disaccord. You will have a bad sound. It is disunity. If you play the right notes we have harmony and unity. A church is filled with different notes, but they can all play together in the right order and have harmony. Most songs are composed of three to five chords. Some have many more. It does not matter how many chords the song has, so long as all the notes are in the chord, and all the chords follow the right order. Co-laboring, not conflict, is the goal of the church. *1Corinthians 14:40 Let all things be done decently and in order.* Yes, there may be different notes in the church, but they are always the right notes. The differences can never be doctrinal. Doctrine is conviction not preference. Preferences are what we hold.

Convictions are what hold us. The right notes will always have sound doctrine. If the trumpet blows an uncertain sound, it will bring destruction and disunity to the church.

We are to be like-minded. This does not speak of our mental aptitude as much as it does our mental attitude. Christians ought to have the same mental attitude. Most great achievements- and sometimes even more so physical attainments- are first won by a strong mental attitude. Diseases of the mind are the great diseases of our day. In verse five we learn that our mind is to be as the mind of Christ. In verse three we learn that it is a lowly mind. Verse seven teaches us that it is the mind of a servant. In verse eight we are shown that the mind of Christ is a mind of humility. Many folks are not interested in obtaining the mind of Christ as they are giving everyone a piece of their own mind. We think that everyone should come around to our way of thinking. To bring our mind into the church, where the mind of Christ is supposed to rule, is to bring a double mind into the church. The Bible tells us that a double minded man is unstable in all his ways. The same is true of a double minded church.

If verse two is not practically applied, the first phrase of verse three will be the result. Strife and vain glory will abound in a church that does not follow the example of her Savior by humbling itself. Disunity is a breeding ground and a battle ground for strife and envy. Much trouble in the church today is not doctrinal as much as it is dispositional. Communist governments have not closed the doors of nearly as many churches as strife and envy have. *Matthew 5:9 Blessed*

are the peacemakers: for they shall be called the children of God.
Today, you would think that God's house was filled not with God's children but with God's enemies. Let us be true children of God. Let us be peacemakers in the church and not a bunch of nit-picking, self-willed, rabble-rousers who are destroying the kingdom of God that Christ came to build. People do not always see eye to eye. The way for a church to get along, in spite of all our differences, is to have a lowly mind. How often do we esteem others better than ourselves? Let me ask it this way: When is the last time you conceded that what someone else thought was worth esteeming above your thoughts? We are to esteem others better than ourselves. This is a hallmark of Christian unity. Pride says I am better than others- my needs come first. Lowliness of mind says that the other guy's opinion is just as good as mine, so I will yield to him. Great military leaders often have denied themselves good rations. They ate what their men ate. If their men did not eat, neither did they. They were expressing lowliness of mind. Have you ever gone without so some other family in the church could have something? We are not talking about major doctrinal differences. Again, doctrinal issues are not the problem in most churches. It is the day to day practical duties and responsibilities of the church, where there are (as Paul told the church at Corinth) differences of administrations and diversities of operations, but the same God which worketh all in all.

It is only when you compare what you know yourself to be with what you think others are, that you become absolutely humble. ~F.B. Meyer

The paradigm of Christ was others. Others was the overpowering and dominating example in the life of our Lord. I have often said, that if anyone could go to the gospels and show me one thing that Jesus did for Himself, I would eat my hat. Jesus never did anything for Himself when He lived on this earth. Everything He did was for others. Jesus was made flesh for others. He lived for others. He died for others. He rose from the dead for others. He reigns eternally for others. He is coming again for others. This is the sum of the Law of God. We love our God by loving others. I love the old song *Others*.

Others
Lord, help me live from day to day
In such a self-forgetful way
That even when I kneel to pray
My prayer shall be for—Others.

Others, Lord, yes others,
Let this my motto be,
Help me to live for others,
That I may live like Thee.

Help me in all the work I do
To ever be sincere and true
And know that all I'd do for You
Must needs be done for—Others.

Let self be crucified and slain
And buried deep: and all in vain
May efforts be to rise again,
Unless to live for—Others.

And when my work on earth is done,
And my new work in Heav'n's begun,

May I forget the crown I've won,
While thinking still of—Others.

It has been said that verses five through eleven are the greatest and the most moving verses that Paul was ever inspired to write about Jesus. Paul knew that the basis for the exaltation of Jesus Christ was based upon the humiliation of Jesus Christ. It was a theme inspired by the Holy Spirit in many of Paul's epistles. *2 Corinthians 8:9 For ye know the grace of our Lord Jesus Christ, that, though he was rich, yet for your sakes he became poor, that ye through his poverty might be rich.* If only we could fully grasp how highly exalted Christ is, and how truly low He became for us! His humility is as high as we have yet to ascend.

Only when we ascend to His glory in heaven will we have any comprehension of His humility on our behalf.

In verses five through eight, we are given the <u>Seven Steps of our Savior's Humiliation.</u>

1. He was consecrated to humble Himself- verse 5.
2. He laid aside a divine body- verse 6.
3. He made Himself of no reputation- verse 7.
4. He took the form of a servant- verse 7.
5. He was made in the likeness of men- verse 7.
6. He humbled Himself- verse 8.
7. He became obedient unto death- verse 8.

We are to have the same mind within us that is found in the mind of Jesus. This is the mind of *kenosis* which we will learn more about in verse seven, but which Paul immediately begins to describe in verse six. In order for you and I to have the mind of Christ, we must understand that we obtain His mind through the mindset Christ had when He walked the earth. The one thing that identifies the mind of Christ and the mind of a true Christian is humility. It is not in our human nature to be humble. When Christ saves us, He imparts to us the divine nature. Now we may truly be like Him, if we will truly become humble ourselves under His Holy Spirit's guidance.

Who, being in the form of God... the Greek word for "being" here describes the very essence of an individual that cannot be changed.

God has always been, and always will be, and there is no changing that fact. There are two Greek words for the word "form"- *morphe* and *schema*. *Morphe* is the essential form that never changes. *Malachi 3:6 For I am the LORD, I change not...Schema* is the outward form, which continually changes from time to time depending upon circumstance. For instance, we are born as a baby, but we are changed as we grow through our toddler, juvenile, adult and elder years. We are always the same person- *morphe*- but our outward form changes with age- *schema.* The Greek word used here is *morphe.* The outward form of Jesus changed- *schema*- when He became a man, but He became a man without every ceasing to be God- *morphe.* God inspired the Scriptures to make sure that the deity of Christ was not changed. The essence of Christ as God the Son was and is intact and unchangeable. It was only the outward form of God that changed when Christ was made in the likeness of men by taking a human body. Colossians tells us that Jesus *is the image of the invisible God, the firstborn of every creature.*

Paul also describes Jesus to us in this way: *Hebrews 1:3 Who being the brightness of his glory, and the express image of his person, and upholding all things by the word of his power, when he had by himself purged our sins, sat down on the right hand of the Majesty on high...*Jesus existed as God in eternity past. That is His unchanging form. He came into the existence of a man and entered a sin-cursed world. No creature could exist in the form of God. Man is made in God's image and likeness, but man cannot have God's divine form, rights or privileges. Man will never be omniscient, omnipresent nor omnipotent. Even in a fully sanctified and glorified body, which we will one day receive, man will never have that form of God. That is what Lucifer aspired to be and was what caused him to be cast out of heaven. Adam aspired to be as God when he ate of the tree of knowledge of good and evil and also fell. Satan lied to Adam and Eve by telling them they would be as gods. Jesus was in the form of God because He was, is, and eternally shall be God's only begotten Son. Jesus, as the eternal Son, was in the form of God's divine being before coming to the earth.

*...thought it not robbery to be equal with God...*The word robbery used here is the Greek word *hapargamos.* It obviously means to steal or to plunder. There is a difference between a thief and a robber. A thief steals when no one is looking. A robber comes in and physically steals before your very eyes. A thief is a sneak. A robber is bold. A robber is willing to not just steal, but to kill and destroy. No one can steal from God for His eye is on all. Jesus could not steal from His Father that which was not rightfully His. It was not robbery for Jesus to be equal with God. The equality of God the Son with God the Father is a gift from the Father to His Son. Here is an oft asked question that is answered in verses six: Was Jesus God? Or was Jesus just like God? That word robbery means "something to be snatched at." Jesus did not have to snatch His deity. It was His. He did not take equality from God or strive to hold on to it. Jesus was not clinging to Himself and His rights as God the Son, when He took the likeness of man and the form of a servant. Jesus did not take His equality wrongfully, because it was

always His rightfully. *John 1:1 In the beginning was the Word, and the Word was with God, and the Word was God.* Jesus said, *I and my Father are One.* Jesus also told us, *Ye believe in God, believe also in me.* Jesus also prayed for the saints that we would be one with Him and the Father, as He and the Father are one- *John 17:21-23 That they all may be one; as thou, Father, art in me, and I in thee, that they also may be one in us: that the world may believe that thou hast sent me. And the glory which thou gavest me I have given them; that they may be one, even as we are one: I in them, and thou in me, that they may be made perfect in one; and that the world may know that thou hast sent me, and hast loved them, as thou hast loved me.* Jesus was with His Father from the beginning and has always been equal to Him. There was never any danger that Christ would lose His position with the Father. No one else could take the place of God the Son.

Jesus *...made himself of no reputation...* Those five words form the one single Greek word *kenosis.* Most theologians term this passage of Scripture as, *"The Kenosis of Christ."* The word *kenosis* simply means "emptying" or "to drain." Christ emptied Himself, or made vain, or of none effect, certain things when He came to this earth. He divested (denied) Himself of something. What was it? It was not His deity for He acknowledged it openly. Many claim that when Jesus became a man He ceased to be God. They claim His humanity demanded that Christ empty Himself of His deity. To claim that Jesus denied His deity, is to claim that His knowledge was no more than any other man of His day. This takes the testimony of the Scripture's inspiration and makes the Bible just another book by just another man. Those who deny the deity of Christ claim that He was not as competent to speak as the Old Testament writers. They claim that without divine knowledge, Jesus had no authority. They would be right if that were true, but it is not. Jesus did not empty Himself of His deity in order to take on humanity. Jesus never denied His deity one time in the Bible. In fact, Peter and many others were sure that Jesus was the Christ, the Son of the living God. Ignorant and unlearned people accept truth by simple faith that many have denied by poor but seemingly higher education. Jesus then said to Peter...*Blessed art thou, Simon Barjona: for flesh and blood hath not revealed it unto thee, but my Father which is in heaven.*

Jesus simply denied Himself of certain rights and certain prerogatives, as God the Son, during the hours of His humanity.

Jesus chose subjection rather than sovereignty. He chose servanthood as opposed to being served. Remember when Jesus was tempted by Satan? He could have turned the stones to bread and called ten thousand angels lest He dashed His foot against a stone. Jesus denied Himself His rights as God the Son, in order to be the Son of Man. Hebrews 4:15 tells us that Jesus was...*tempted in all points like as we are, yet without sin.*

He also emptied Himself of His glory. Jesus veiled His heavenly glory while on the earth. He kept it hidden behind the veil of His flesh. When the Word became flesh, the Shekinah glory was shrouded. Only when His earthly work was at an end was He glorified. Even then, only a few saw it on the Mount of Transfiguration. It was all voluntary on His part.

...and took upon him the form of a servant. Jesus is the King of kings and Lord of lords, yet He never made any claim to it while in the days of His flesh. He was born into a lowly peasant family. Joseph and Mary were honest and hardworking but very humble. He was born into the home of servants, and thus Jesus was even more able to take a servant's form. Here is that word "form" again. Yet again, it is the word *morphe.* Servanthood is the very nature and unchanging essence of God the Son. *Mark 10:45 For even the Son of man came not to be ministered unto, but to minister, and to give his life a ransom for many.* Jesus came to serve, and He continues to serve even now. *Romans 8:34 Who [is] he that condemneth? [It is] Christ that died, yea rather, that is risen again, who is even at the right hand of God, who also maketh intercession for us. Hebrews 7:25 Wherefore he is able also to save them to the uttermost that come unto God by him, seeing he ever liveth to make intercession for them.*

...and was made in the likeness of men. The word likeness simply means "resemblance." Jesus needed to know the experiences of the human life. He had to experience pain, sickness, hunger, thirst and temptation. He had to feel our infirmities in order to be a good and truly merciful High Priest to us. *Hebrews 4:15 For we have not an high priest which cannot be touched with the feeling of our infirmities; but was in all points tempted like as we are, yet without sin.* Jesus took a human form to resemble mankind. Jesus did not come with the best

physique or the most handsome face in order to flaunt Himself. Vanity was not His nature. Humility was. Jesus was so much like the common man, that He could disappear into a crowd and never be found. He was totally unobtrusive. *Isaiah 53:2 For he shall grow up before him as a tender plant, and as a root out of a dry ground: he hath no form nor comeliness; and when we shall see him, there is no beauty that we should desire him.* Can you imagine what it would be like if you and I had to humble ourselves to be made into the likeness of a stink bug? Now try to imagine God humbling Himself by taking on a body of humanity.

*And being found in fashion as a man...*The word fashion is the word *schema* that we spoke of earlier. Jesus not only resembled men; His fashion was the same as man. He did not come to the earth as a fully mature man. He was fashioned in the womb of Mary. Jesus divested Himself of His celestial body in exchange for a terrestrial body. *Luke 2:52 And Jesus increased in wisdom and stature, and in favour with God and man.* Jesus went through all of the experiences of infancy, childhood, adolescence and adulthood.

...he humbled himself... No one had to humble Jesus. No one could humble Jesus. He humbled Himself. There are those who have to be humbled by God, and there are those who humble themselves before God. The latter is far better than the former, and here in these three words lies one of the greatest lessons on humility.

...and became obedient unto death, even the death of the cross. The culmination of Christ's humility was Calvary. Each step of

humiliation took Jesus deeper to His final point of humiliation on Calvary, where He was laid to an open shame. Jesus went from a throne of glory to a tree on Golgotha. He died for sin, having no need to pay the wages of sin, since He was sinless. In His humility, He even chose a form of death reserved for slaves and common criminals who had no Roman citizenship. Roman law dictated that a Roman citizen could never be crucified. That is why Paul, as a Roman citizen, was beheaded. He was given what was considered a quick and a clean death, instead of the slow, agonizing death of the cross. This is fitting for a sinner, but humiliating for God. *2 Corinthians 5:21 For he hath made him to be sin for us, who knew no sin; that we might be made the righteousness of God in him. 1 Peter 2:24 Who his own self bare our sins in his own body on the tree, that we, being dead to sins, should live unto righteousness: by whose stripes ye were healed.* There was a great distance between the throne and the tree. Only the love, humility and service of Christ could span and measure that distance. We are given Scripture to observe it in order to catch a glimpse of true humility. Whatever humility we shall descend to, it will not be as far as Christ came for us. We are all going to die. Will you die humble? Are you willing to die in order to obtain the culmination of humility? If we are going to help this world come to God, we must be willing to humble ourselves as servants. There is no other way to sit with Christ on His throne of eternal glory. Let this mind be in you.

Rejoice In Christ's Paradigm Of Majesty- Philippians 2:9-11

Philippians 2:9-11 *Wherefore God also hath highly exalted him, and given him a name which is above every name: That at the name of Jesus every knee should bow, of things in heaven, and things in earth, and things under the earth; And that every tongue should confess that Jesus Christ is Lord, to the glory of God the Father.*

There is no passage where the extremes of our Saviour's majesty and humility are brought into such abrupt connection. Guided by the Spirit of God, the Apostle opens the golden compasses of his imagination and faith, and places the one point upon the supernal Throne of the eternal God, and the other upon the Cross of shame where Jesus died, and he shows us the great steps by which Jesus approached always nearer and nearer to human sin and need; that, having embraced us in our low estate, He might carry us back with Himself to the very bosom of God, and that by identifying Himself with our sin and sorrow He might ultimately identify us with the glory which He had with the Father before the world was. ~F.B. Meyer

These verses are the fulfillment of Psalm 110. *Psalms 110:1-7 <<A Psalm of David.>> The LORD said unto my Lord, Sit thou at my right hand, until I make thine enemies thy footstool. The LORD shall send the rod of thy strength out of Zion: rule thou in the midst of thine enemies. Thy people shall be willing in the day of thy power, in the beauties of holiness from the womb of the morning: thou hast the dew of thy youth.*

The LORD hath sworn, and will not repent, Thou art a priest for ever after the order of Melchizedek. The Lord at thy right hand shall strike through kings in the day of his wrath. He shall judge among the heathen, he shall fill the places with the dead bodies; he shall wound the heads over many countries. He shall drink of the brook in the way: therefore shall he lift up the head. The man, Christ Jesus, humbled Himself, and was exalted by God. As Zechariah declares, He is "Jehovah's Fellow." In verses nine through eleven we find our Savior's seven steps of Exaltation:

1. God the Father highly exalted Him- verse 9.
2. God the Father gave Him a name above every name- verse 9.
3. At the name of Jesus every knee must bow- verse 10.
4. Everything in heaven must bow- verse 10.
5. Everything in earth- verse 10.
6. Everything under the earth- verse 10.
7. Every tongue must confess His Lordship to the glory of God the Father- verse 11.

The New Testament repeatedly reminds us of the difference between the actions of men and the actions of God concerning Jesus. Ephesians 1:15-23 is a fitting passage to read alongside of these verses. Wicked men crucified the Prince of glory. God the Father raised Him from the dead and exalted Him. It is worthy to note that once Jesus cried "It is finished" from the cross, there was not another act of desecration committed against His body. The disciples tenderly took the body of our Savior and Lord down from the cross, carefully embalmed Him and laid Him sorrowfully in a tomb.

It is important to be reminded once again that whenever Paul wrote of Jesus that his intention was not just to teach us *about* Jesus but to instruct us how to be *like* Jesus. Paul's desire was for the Philippians to live in such a way that discord, disunity and personal ambitions would have no place in the church. Paul used the humility and the exaltation of Christ to teach the Philippians (and all church members ever after) to concern ourselves with our humility and let God exalt whom He will when He wishes. *1 Peter 5:6 Humble yourselves therefore under the mighty hand of God, that he may exalt you in due time.*

It has been said that it is of infinite importance to know what God loves best that we might love it too. We are going to live with God eternally. It is imperative that we know that ideal which God most cherishes, that we might also cherish it too and thus endear ourselves to our heavenly Father. If we know this ideal and live by it, we can be fashioned into the image and glory of Christ. We may be drawn to the bosom of God as friends and dear children. The name that is dearest to God is Jesus. The ideal that dominated the life of Jesus is humility. Humility is what God exalts. When our Lord walked this earth His desire was not to dominate the world but to serve it. Jesus won the hearts of those who believed on Him not by force of power but by His love, service and sacrifice. This model of character should be the

103

pursuit of every Christian. The old hymn writer Isaac Watts wrote of it
this way:

> *When I survey the wondrous cross*
> *On which the Prince of glory died,*
> *My richest gain I count but loss,*
> *And pour contempt on all my pride.*

Jesus did not seek His will but His Father's will. The humility of
Christ brought Him a greater glory. True worship is based on love and
sacrifice not fear.

Jesus humbled Himself and His Father exalted Him higher than ever
before. Jesus humbled Himself to the death of the cross on Calvary.
Now the Father assures both Christ and all who have ever lived on the
Lord's earth that there is coming a day when every knee shall bow to
Him. Christ has never had a day like this, but it is a day that will come
to Him. Christ made it His business to humble Himself and the Father
made it His business to exalt His Son. This is a good lesson for Christians
and is taught to us by our Lord Himself throughout the gospel records
and repeated by apostles. We would all do well to concern ourselves
with humbling ourselves and let God exalt us if He so desires. *Matthew
23:12 And whosoever shall exalt himself shall be abased; and he that
shall humble himself shall be exalted. Luke 14:11 For whosoever
exalteth himself shall be abased; and he that humbleth himself shall be
exalted. Luke 18:14 I tell you, this man went down to his house justified*

rather than the other: for every one that exalteth himself shall be abased; and he that humbleth himself shall be exalted. James 4:10 Humble yourselves in the sight of the Lord, and he shall lift you up. 1Peter 5:6 Humble yourselves therefore under the mighty hand of God, that he may exalt you in due time... 2 Corinthians 8:9 For ye know the grace of our Lord Jesus Christ, that, though he was rich, yet for your sakes he became poor, that ye through his poverty might be rich. No one ever was ever richer than Jesus Christ. No one ever became poorer. No matter how much you have to give, you will never sacrifice as Jesus has. No matter how little you have, you will never be poorer. Jesus owned it all to give it all.

God gave to His Son *the* name that is above every name. There are names above names in the annals of earthly history: Alexander the Great, Antiochus Epiphanies, Hannibal, Caesar Augustus, Napoleon Bonaparte, George Washington, Abraham Lincoln, Stalin, Lenin, Karl Marx, Hitler, Bin Laden, William Tyndale, John Wycliffe, John Huss, John Knox, Moses, Elijah, David, Paul, Peter, James, John. There is not enough space for names that have risen to the top of every generation. Some names are good and some are evil, but there is a name that is above every name that has ever been. That is the name of Jesus. All of history is His story. He is the hinge of all our time. He is the Door that leads from heaven to earth and back to heaven again. The name of Jesus is the name that is above every name. Probably my favorite poem in all the world is this one called *The Incomparable Christ.*

The Incomparable Christ

2,000 years ago there was born a man contrary to the laws of life and the rules of nature.

He lived in poverty and was reared in obscurity.

He never traveled extensively. Only crossing the boundary of the country in which He lived one time and that during early childhood.

He possessed neither wealth nor influence.

His parents were inconspicuous and uninfluential and had neither training nor education.

In infancy He startled a king.

In childhood He puzzled the doctors.

In manhood He ruled the course of nature walking upon the billows as if they were pavement and hushing the seas to sleep.

He never wrote a book, yet all the libraries of the world cannot contain the books that are written about Him.

He never wrote a song, yet He has
furnished the theme for more songs
than all the songwriters in the world's
history combined.
He never founded a college, yet all the
colleges combined cannot boast of
having as many students as He does.
He never practiced medicine and yet He
has healed more broken hearts and sick
bodies than all the doctors of the world
combined.
He never marshaled an army, fired a
gun or drafted a soldier, yet no general
has had more volunteers under His
orders who has caused more rebels to
stack arms and surrender without a shot
ever being fired.
Every 7th day the wheels of commerce
cease to move and multitudes flood into
His house to pay homage and respect
unto Him.
The names of past proud statesman of
Greece and Rome have come and gone,
yet the name of this Man lives on.

Though 2,000 years has separated this

congregation and the scene of His

crucifixion He still lives.

Herod could not kill Him. Satan could

not seduce Him. Death could not

destroy Him, and the grave couldn't hold

Him.

He stands forth upon the highest

pinnacle of heavenly glory proclaimed of

God, acknowledged by angels and

adored by the saints of God and feared

by the imps of hell.

He is the Ancient of Days!

He is alive and He lives forevermore!

He is set down at the right hand of the

Father, and He liveth to ever make

intercession for us!

~Author Unknown~

In Leviticus 12 we find the Jewish custom of naming a son and the purifying of the mother. In Luke 2 we have the record of Jesus being named and brought to the temple as well. *Luke 2:21-22 And when eight days were accomplished for the circumcising of the child, his name was called JESUS, which was so named of the angel before he was conceived in the womb. And when the days of her purification* *according to the law of Moses were accomplished, they brought him to Jerusalem, to present him to the Lord...*The mother of a Jewish son was purified after seven days. Seven is the Bible number of completion, perfection and maturity. On the eighth day (the number of new beginnings) the son was circumcised and his name was announced to all by the son's father. In another 33 days (now 40 days after the birth) the child was taken to the temple and there his name was once again announced and officially entered into the records of the temple and/or the local synagogue. Joseph did not choose the name of Jesus. God the Father sent an angel to Joseph to tell him what name to call Jesus- Matthew 1:20-25. The Father named the Son. Joseph was given the privilege of pronouncing the name of Jesus. Only one man in the history of the world was given the honor of pronouncing the name of Jesus to his family and in the temple. God exalted a humble carpenter with that privilege. There is no way to divine exaltation without humility.

Remember, that when the name of Jesus was proclaimed on the eighth day it was a time of new beginnings. It was a new name in the effect that the name of Jesus is now a name above every name. Oftentimes in the Bible, folks were given new names for new beginnings in life. The name of Abram was changed to Abraham. Jacob's name was changed to Israel. All the saints of God will be given a new name in heaven- Revelation 2:17. Why will we be given new names? God is going to make new heavens and a new earth. The former heavens and earth will pass away never to enter into our minds again. A new life yields a new name. The name of Jesus foreshadowed salvation to both Jews and Greeks. Jesus is the Greek name for the Old Testament name Joshua which is an abbreviated form of Jehovah-*Yeshua*. The name Jesus means "Jehovah saves from sin." There has never been a name like the name of Jesus. Beloved, let us reverence the name of Jesus. The world blasphemes that name. There must be those who reverence, cherish and speak it in love. The name of Jesus will be the last name spoken on earth and the first name uttered in heaven. The name of Jesus describes to us all we know of love, selflessness, humility and sacrifice. It is the spelling of God's mercy, grace and glory. Only an infantile percentage of the world has ever loved, respected and revered that name. Most use it as a name of blasphemy. Indeed, in the world in which we now live, the name of Jesus is more likely to be heard spoken in blasphemy than in any other context. You hear His name blasphemed in the work place. You hear it blasphemed on the television. The world never swears by the names of their gods. They never blaspheme the names of pagan deities. Every time the world blasphemes the name of Jesus, they are despitefully acknowledging His Lordship over them.

Jesus will be called Lord by all in heaven, in earth and from hell beneath the earth. The word Lord has a rich history. In the Old Testament you will often see the word lord spelled "LORD." It is totally capitalized, but the first letter is larger than the rest. It is the name of Jehovah God. In the New Testament the word lord is the Greek word *kurios*. It began by being defined as "master" or "owner." It later became the official title of Roman emperors. It also became the title of the Greek and Roman gods. For the Christian, the Hebrews word for Jehovah- *Yahweh*- was translated into the Greek New Testament as *kurios*- Lord. Jesus is the master and owner of all life. This title makes Him King of kings and Lord of all lords, but in a way that no emperor or pagan god could ever be.

Jesus is not just Lord. He is Jesus Christ our Lord. He is divine deity. There is coming a day of confession when all who are in heaven, on earth and those under the earth (hell) will bow their knees to Jesus and confess Him as Lord. Not everyone will call Jesus "Savior" but all will one day call Him "Lord." Those who know Jesus as their Savior will call Him Lord. Tragically, many of these may have never done so on earth. Those who in the days of their flesh claimed they would never bow before God will all one day bow. This will only add more agony to their eternal torments. Those who called Christ Lord but not Savior will bow. The angels of God will bow. Satan and all the fallen host of heaven will bow. *Isaiah 14:12 How art thou fallen from heaven, O Lucifer, son of the morning! how art thou cut down to the ground, which didst weaken the nations! Isaiah 14:16 They that see thee shall narrowly look upon thee, and consider thee, saying, Is this the man that made the earth to tremble, that did shake kingdoms...*

The Restitutionists take these verses and make claim that one day all will be reconciled to God, and the whole world will be saved. Nothing could be further from the truth. There is an eternal span between subjugation and reconciliation. Bringing all men under

111

subjection to the Lord will not reconcile them to the Savior. Notice very carefully what these verses say. The unbeliever will confess Jesus as Lord not Savior. If you have not claimed Christ as your Savior here, you will only say Lord in heaven. It will be eternally too late. Jesus Himself taught us this in the Sermon on the Mount. *Matthew 7:21-23 Not every one that saith unto me, Lord, Lord, shall enter into the kingdom of heaven; but he that doeth the will of my Father which is in heaven. Many will say to me in that day, Lord, Lord, have we not prophesied in thy name? and in thy name have cast out devils? and in thy name done many wonderful works? And then will I profess unto them, I never knew you: depart from me, ye that work iniquity.* It is tragic that there are countless souls on earth who have claimed Christ as Lord but not Savior. Jesus wants to be both Savior and Lord. In order to have any hope of surviving that great and notable day of the Lord, you must first know Christ as your personal Savior. You can bow now or bow later, but all will one day bow the knee. If you despise the authority of Jesus Christ the Lord on earth, you will be tormented by it in hell for all eternity. There will be no further rebellion in hell. Even in hell, all will be under the authority and government of Jesus. Charles Spurgeon used to preach a very famous sermon called *Turn or Burn.*

If Jesus is your Savior, then He is worthy to be your Lord. Christians should bow to Christ and make Him Lord of their life as they die to self daily. When I bow to Jesus and confess Him as Lord on that day, that will not be the first day of my life to do so, and it should not be so for you either. Christ should daily be enthroned upon the heart of every

Christian. This crucifies the flesh and revives us in the Spirit. Make it a daily habit to bow to Christ in worship and subjection.

On this day, the world will say that *Jesus Christ is Lord, to the glory of God the Father.* The whole work of the Son is to bring glory to His Father. Jesus draws all men to Himself that He might bring them to His Father- John 14:6. Dear child of God, can you say the same? In the church at Philippi there were those who sought to exalt themselves and bring the attention and focus of the church upon themselves. A godly Christian will turn the eyes of the people to Jesus and our heavenly Father.

Rejoice In Christ's Paradigm Of Ministry- Philippians 2:12-16

Philippians 2:12-16 *Wherefore, my beloved, as ye have always obeyed, not as in my presence only, but now much more in my absence, work out your own salvation with fear and trembling. For it is God which worketh in you both to will and to do of his good pleasure. Do all things without murmurings and disputings: That ye may be blameless and harmless, the sons of God, without rebuke, in the midst of a crooked and perverse nation, among whom ye shine as lights in the world; Holding forth the word of life; that I may rejoice in the day of Christ, that I have not run in vain, neither laboured in vain.*

These verses before us refer to our life in the assembly of the church and our personal responsibilities. We find in verses twelve through fourteen that there are six results of being obedient to God:

1. We will be blameless before God.
2. We will be harmless to men.
3. We will be identified as the sons of God.
4. We will be without rebuke by man.
5. We will shine as lights in the world.
6. We will hold forth the Word of life.

As Paul begins this next passage, he reminds the Philippians that they cannot continue to count on him. They must spiritually mature in order to carry on the work of Christ in a Christ-like way even in Paul's absence. Paul, even if released to them, would soon give his life on Nero's chopping block. The church must be ready to continue in the faith in Paul's absence as they did in his presence.

Many have taken this verse out of context by claiming that our salvation is maintained and dependent upon our good works for its sustainment. This verse has often perplexed those who thought they clearly believed that salvation is by grace through faith and that not of works, lest any man should boast. Truly, salvation is dependent on the grace of God from start to finish. Salvation is found in the finished work of Christ, and no man can add to what God has finished. Salvation is Jesus Christ plus nothing- minus nothing. It is both ludicrous and blasphemous to think that any work by any man could put the capstone on the cornerstone laid at Calvary. There is nothing more precious to God than the blood of His Son. His death and blood alone were offered once for all our sins- Hebrews 10:10.

This epistle, more than any other of Paul's, makes the clear distinction between the internal regeneration of salvation and the external work of salvation. James 2 gives us the greatest exposition that distinguishes between the two. Internal salvation is the regeneration of the Holy Spirit through Christ's atonement which results in our justification before God. The external evidence of our salvation is our sanctification which one day will be completely fulfilled at the resurrection when we receive a glorified body like unto His.

You see, God looks on the inside and sees our standing. The world cannot see that. Neither can the church of God. The world and the church look to our state (condition) with God. That is seen by our works. In Romans 3 and 4 we are told that no man can be justified before God by the deeds of the law. God looks on the heart. In James 2 we are told to show men our faith by our works. *James 2:17-18 Even so faith, if it hath not works, is dead, being alone. Yea, a man may say, Thou hast faith, and I have works: shew me thy faith without thy works, and I will shew thee my faith by my works.* God looks at the work that He does in our heart. The world sees God's work in our heart by our outward works done for our Heavenly Father from a grateful heart. Your neighbor cannot see your faith. They can only see the work of your faith. Even the prophet Samuel judged by the outward appearance when he looked on Eliab. *1 Samuel 16:7 But the LORD said unto Samuel, Look not on his countenance, or on the height of his stature; because I have refused him: for the LORD seeth not as man seeth; for man looketh on the outward appearance, but the LORD*

115

looketh on the heart. Man does look on the outward appearance. Yes, there are those who look good outwardly but are inwardly full of dead man's bones. Jesus dealt with these hypocrites in great detail in Matthew 23. Nevertheless, the world needs to see our good works for God as validation of the work that God has done in our hearts. What the world sees must be an honest reflection of what is in your heart.

There is a little story that more than one Bible commentator has used to illustrate the context of this verse. There was a little girl who listened to a pastor preach a legalistic sermon from this very text. The preacher was very insistent that no one could be saved by grace alone, but everyone must work out their own salvation. Very innocently the little girl asked her mother after the service, "Mother, how can you work it out, if you haven't got it in?" Out of the mouths of babes the truth is often spoken in simplicity and sincerity. I do not know if it is a true story or not. It has been reported as true, and it appears to be so for out of the mouth of simple faith often comes the most spiritual sensibility.

Here are a few statements some great men of God made about this verse. One saint of God said, "Faith alone saves, but the faith that saves is not alone." D.L. Moody wrote in his Bible next to this verse, "Unless God has first worked it into you, you cannot work it out." F.B. Meyer said, "If justification were all, God would simply throw white robes on us." Dr. Henry Ironside wrote of this verse, "Notice first, however, that the apostle does not speak of working *for* salvation, but of working it *out*, which is a very different thing." Lehman Strauss once said, "God nowhere is said to call upon an unsaved person to work out a salvation that He has not worked in, but He fully expects the inwrought work of regeneration to be worked out by the regenerated one."

These verses were given to teach the assembly of believers that as we go through life our corrupt nature is going to reveal itself personally and ecclesiastically. We are going to have to continue on in fellowship and service in spite of our faults and failures. The greatest opposition against the church, more often than not, comes from within not from without.

Paul uses the words "fear and trembling" in several places. In 1 Corinthians 2:3, he tells us that he testified in "fear and trembling." He said that Titus was received in "fear and trembling" in 2 Corinthians 7:15. In Ephesians 6:5 he tells servants to obey their masters in "fear and trembling." Here he tells us to work out our salvation in fear and trembling. This is not a warning that we might perish or lose our salvation, but because of the weakness of the flesh, we are to be fearful of turning once again to the ways of the world and the wiles of the Wicked One. The flesh is weak, and our flesh will most certainly fail us. The world criticizes all we do. The Wicked One walks about as a roaring lion seeking whom he may devour. Paul is saying that what is in you will work its way out of you. But be careful, the world and the devil will come after you. Before you belonged to them; now you belong to God. You have abandoned their family, and now, they hate you. They will do all they can to destroy both you and any good work for Christ you do.

The saved man is God's workmanship, but he is also God's workman. We work, and God works. It is a combination and an interaction of God's sovereign grace and power, co-laboring with the free moral agency of man. The Father and the child are co-laborers. God co-labors with both the farmer and the coal miner. God creates the seed that the farmer plants in the ground. God places the coal in the earth, but the miner must get it out. This is God's good pleasure. It pleases God to include us in His work. This is a high honor! God does not have to include us, but He does. Service to God is a privilege not a punishment. Sad, but true, many consider serving the Lord to be a life of hard bondage. God cannot bless the hours of your labor unless it is done with a right heart.

The fatalists all say that whatever is going to be, will be, regardless of what man does. Many Scriptures refute such a claim. 2 Corinthians 9:6 and Galatians 6:8 clearly teach that we have both an eternal and a direct impact on the Lord's work by our own choice. The fatalists claim God will exercise His sovereignty and omnipotence without the surrendered will of man. God is sovereign and omnipotent, but He does not allow His nature to supersede the free will of man. If the fatalists are true, then why does God not eradicate our flesh? Jesus did not come in a glorified body to serve God. He came in a body of flesh just like ours. He did so to prove that God can work in our lives in spite of our earthly condition. Jesus showed us that God can work His will by His power as we yield our flesh unto God. The child of God must surrender to the Father's will in complete obedience. In these verses divine sovereignty and human responsibility meet at a crossroads. The only worthwhile choice is to decide to be obedient to God's will for God's good pleasure. This a distinct trait to Christianity. God dwells in us and works in us, but God does so without eradicating the personality that He has first given us in our natural birth. God is in us, but He does not take from us the individuality or the free will that He has first granted us. He comes along side and brings us together. He uses our personality, but He performs His good will. God works His will in our lives as we submit to Him. For example, God used Isaiah, but He still allowed Isaiah to be Isaiah. He used Jeremiah who was distinctly different from Isaiah, because God allowed Jeremiah to be Jeremiah. John was not like Peter at all, and no one was like John the Baptist. God uses our individuality and personality to perform His holy work in our lives. Paul explained this truth to the church of Corinth as well. *1 Corinthians 15:10 But by the grace of God I am what I am: and his grace which was bestowed upon me was not in vain; but I laboured more abundantly than they all: yet not I, but the grace of God which was with me.* Paul had accomplished more than all the other apostles. This was not a statement of pride or arrogance. It was a statement of the work of Christ according to God's good pleasure. It was not a lie, or God would not have allowed it to be recorded in Scripture. God had a great work and needed someone like Paul to do it. God created the man for the work and the work for the man. Humility accepts you and God's will for your life without coveting what God has for someone else.

How do I know if God is working His will in me? F.B. Meyer gave three ways that we know that God's will is done within us. *"First, there must be a holy discontent with yourself. We must be dissatisfied with all we have ever done in our own efforts. Second, we must aspire. We must look above the snow-capped peaks, and your heart longs to climb and to stand there. Third, you have the appreciation for the possibility that you can be blameless and without rebuke...When the Spirit of God lives within you, there rises up a consciousness that you have the capacity for the highest possible attainments, because you were made and redeemed in the image of God, and because the germ of the Christ-nature has been sown in your spirit."*

Philippi was the best of churches, but even the best of churches have their troubles. Seeds of rivalry and discord were beginning to be planted. Paul knew these must be dealt with quickly lest they become deep rooted and destructive. It has been said that when a horse begins to kick, he has stopped pulling. The same truth applies to church members. Murmuring is quarreling with God. It means "to grumble." It seems there are those who always grumble and complain. These are the folks who are always against the things the church is doing to advance the gospel. They can never provide a solution or an alternative measure, but they can point out all the problems. Nothing will be done for Christ without problems. We live in an imperfect world. We must continue to rise above and conquer our problems.

The children of Israel murmured twenty-six times during their forty year wandering in the wilderness. Murmuring provoked God to anger more than anything else. There are not many times that you see God destroying people in the Bible. God did not destroy Cain for killing Abel, yet God did destroy His own people for murmuring. God destroyed the world of Noah for their atheism. God destroyed Sodom and Gomorrha for their great immorality. God places murmuring next to the sins of sodomy and atheism. That is a sober warning to us all. Paul also warned the church at Corinth about this. *1 Corinthians 10:10-12 Neither murmur ye, as some of them also murmured, and were destroyed of the destroyer. Now all these things happened unto them for ensamples: and they are written for our admonition, upon whom the ends of the world are come. Wherefore let him that thinketh he standeth take heed lest he fall.* Murmuring implies that you can do it better than God. A murmuring Christian has never been of any good use to God. Keep your heart and tongue right before God. James tells us that no man can tame his own tongue. It is a world of iniquity and it is set on fire of hell, but the Holy Spirit lives in you. He can tame it. Listen to Him. When He says keep quiet, bite your tongue. When He says speak, speak only what He tells you, and remember, God will never cause you to speak contrary to His word or to bring disunity to the church. God never commands us to speak in pride to promote our point.

If murmuring against God continues in the church, the church will doubtless come to disputing among themselves. Disputing means "discussion." Disputing is quarreling with men. These churches have traded pastoral oversight and submissive service for committees. They have lots of meetings. They discuss many things. Typically, all they do is create personality clashes and attempt personal conquests. It is about who is right and not what is right. Korah held a committee meeting and God swallowed him, his family and his entire committee alive into the pit of hell. Even God hates committees. Committees discuss things, but they never do anything. It is only after we have laid aside our murmuring and disputing that we can claim such godly character before God.

Those who live according to verse fourteen have no claim to the godly character of verse fifteen. God wants us to be blameless. We should be blameless before both God and men. Let us not be found at fault in the murmuring and disputing that seems to be found in every church. We are only blameless if we have no part. No blame can be placed on those uninvolved. Euodias and Syntyche were involved in disputation. Those not involved with the quarrel between these two women were blameless. The blameless should also be harmless. Harm comes *to* all, but harm should never come *from* God's own. It has been well said that if we would keep our hearts right towards God inwardly then we will be right with all others outwardly. Guard the inner man and keep the secret places of the heart pure.

Being blameless does not teach that our standing as sons of God is determined by our works, but rather that our state is determined by our works. Zacharias and Elisabeth walked before God in all the commandments and ordinances of the Lord. If we will be obedient to God in all His ways, we may be blameless before all. Those who are blameless and harmless will be the sons of God without rebuke. The words "without rebuke" also mean "without blemish or defect." The lambs that were offered every morning and every evening on the brazen altar had to be without blemish. Paul told the church at Ephesus that when Christ calls His bride from out of this world that He will...*present it to himself a glorious church, not having spot, or wrinkle, or any such thing; but that it should be holy and without blemish.* 1 John 3 tells us that we are to be pure even as He also is pure. Paul echoes the command of Christ given in the Sermon on the Mount. *Matthew 5:16 Let your light so shine before men, that they may see your good works, and glorify your Father which is in heaven.* As children we used to sing the song "This Little Light of Mine." Our life is to be a light. Jesus warned us against hiding it under a bushel. As the stars shine in the heavens and give light to the night, so we are to let our lights shine in this dark world. As the moon gives no light of her own but reflects the light of the sun to give the greater light to the night, so also should we reflect the light of the Son of God. In   a crooked and perverse world, this seems to be an impossible task, but it is not impossible. With God all things are possible. Nothing is too hard for the Lord. I grow weary of those who use the pitiful condition of this present world as an excuse for their laziness and their cowardice. How can we possibly shine as lights in this world? The answer is found in the next verse.

Life and light are related. Life grows from the light. We get our word "photo" from this Greek word for light. It means "brilliant" or "illumination."   In the natural world this process is called photosynthesis. In Photosynthesis a plant draws the light of the sun and makes-synthesizes-food from carbon dioxide and water. Photosynthesis in plants generally involves the green pigment chlorophyll and generates oxygen as a byproduct. What makes up the light that brings life? It is the holding forth of the Word of Life. Light produces growth. Our light should produce new life. Even under the Old Covenant the Bible teaches us that our light and the life of men are yoked together. *Daniel 12:3 And they that be wise shall shine as the brightness of the firmament; and they that turn many to righteousness as the stars for ever and ever.* John spoke of Jesus as both the light and the life of men. *John 1:1-5 In the beginning was the Word, and the Word was with God, and the Word was God. The same was in the beginning with God. All things were made by him; and without him was not any thing made that was made. In him was life; and the life was the light of men. And the light shineth in darkness; and the darkness comprehended it not.* Here is something every child of God can and should do. Far too many try to disqualify themselves because of their weaknesses. They try to hide behind their lack of education or a poor way with people or perhaps their shy spirit. We have a command from God, and behind all of God's commands God places His omnipotence. When God calls, He qualifies us. Moses was a stutterer and Paul's speech was contemptible. Those two men are the greatest voices of

124

the Old and New Testaments in spite of their inadequacies and inabilities. We should hold forth the Word of Life. We can take the light of God's Word and the glorious gospel of Christ, and shine it forth into the darkness and depravity of this world. The church is to combine its efforts and resources into an all-out effort to proclaim the gospel to every creature. Those who are occupied in verse sixteen will not fall into the condemnation that awaits those in verse fourteen. What a sober responsibility it is to live for Christ!

Paul makes a reference here likening his labor to running a race. It was often the custom of Paul to relate the spiritual life to things correlative in the natural life. He often used physical engagements like running, boxing, wrestling and soldiering to make his point. This parallel is not out of context. The Roman Gymnasium was used for more than just sport. It was not just athletics that were featured there. Historians, poets, philosophers and sculptors all came to reveal their latest works. Sophists (professors of philosophy), philosophers (the pupils of philosophy) and preachers all found audience in the Gymnasium. Socrates discussed eternity in the Gymnasium. Many schools have their commencement exercises or banquets in the Gymnasium as well.

Typically, we first think of sports to be the gymnasium's general purpose today. The Greeks had three great athletic events. The Isthmian Games were held annually at Corinth. The Pan-Ionian games were held annually at Ephesus, and, of course, the Olympic games were held every four years in Athens. The foot race was the most famous event of all that transpired in the Gymnasium. Paul wrote of the herald calling the starters to the line- 1 Corinthians 9:27. He had seen the runners press towards their mark- Philippians 3:14. He had seen the winner awarded the prize- Philippians 3:14; 2 Timothy 4:8. He wrote also of the victor's laurel crown- 1 Corinthians 9:24; Philippians 4:1. He spoke of the strict discipline and training that was undertaken by the runners- 1 Timothy 4:7-8; 2 Timothy 2:5. Paul's prayer was that he would not be like the athlete who went through all the labor and sacrifice only to lose. He did not want the work he had done for Christ to count for nothing. His great prize would be for those whom he had loved to continue in their love and service for Christ. No man lives unto himself, and no man dies unto himself. Paul truly saw earthly relationships continuing eternally in heaven. He wanted the church at Philippi to do well so that his labor would not be in vain. All rejoicing in the day of Christ is based on our fruitfulness for Christ.

Rejoice In Christ's Paradigm Of Messengers- Philippians 2:17-30

Philippians 2:17-30 *Yea, and if I be offered upon the sacrifice and service of your faith, I joy, and rejoice with you all. For the same cause also do ye joy, and rejoice with me. But I trust in the Lord Jesus to send Timotheus shortly unto you, that I also may be of good comfort, when I know your state. For I have no man likeminded, who will naturally care for your state. For all seek their own, not the things which are Jesus Christ's. But ye know the proof of him, that, as a son with the father, he hath served with me in the gospel. Him therefore I hope to send* *presently, so soon as I shall see how it will go with me. But I trust in the Lord that I also myself shall come shortly. Yet I supposed it necessary to send to you Epaphroditus, my brother, and companion in labour, and fellowsoldier, but your messenger, and he that ministered to my wants. For he longed after you all, and was full of heaviness, because that ye had heard that he had been sick. For indeed he was sick nigh unto death: but God had mercy on him; and not on him only, but on me also, lest I should have sorrow upon sorrow. I sent him therefore the more carefully, that, when ye see him again, ye may rejoice, and that I may be the less sorrowful. Receive him therefore in the Lord with all gladness; and hold such in reputation: Because for the work of Christ he was nigh unto death, not regarding his life, to supply your lack of service toward me.*

We have been learning of both lowliness and light in this chapter. Christ is our greatest paradigm for both; however, the Scriptures reveal to us that both lowliness and light are attainable for God's people. Three great human examples lie before us: Paul, Timothy and Epaphroditus. All three of these men followed the paradigm of the mind of Christ. They are set forth as ensamples for us to follow. We may follow them as they followed Christ. It has been said that the Bible is so divine because it is so human. This chapter begins with the Man of Sorrows and closes with the sorrow of the man- the Apostle Paul.

Paul

Paul was a leader of men and a lover of all who followed him in Christ Jesus. It is not likely that there has ever been a greater New Testament leader than Paul. In his declaration of devotion to the Philippians, Timothy, and Epaphroditus, we find another secret to Paul's success. Paul did not sing his own praises. He praised his fellow helpers in the Lord. He knew that the work that was credited to him was made possible by the sacrifice of those that serve quietly in the shadows.

We may count it a settled thing that no man can be a great leader of men who has no power to draw a following. And no man can long hold the following he draws whose selfishness does not allow him to recognize and appreciate the merits of his followers. ~B.H. Carroll

Paul's life was one of continual sacrifice. He was truly a living sacrifice, just as he wrote in Romans 12. He constantly showed his compassion and pastoral care for the flock of God at Philippi. It is possible that no other man ever drank as deep into the Spirit of Christ as Paul did. Paul was once a proud and haughty Pharisee full of self-righteousness. He was a bigot and a persecutor of the church of God. Now, he is the shining example of humility and the apostle of the Gentiles. He judged himself in the light of the cross of His Savior and the power of Christ rested on him. To the elders of Ephesus Paul declared in *Acts 20:24 But none of these things move me, neither count*

I my life dear unto myself, so that I might finish my course with joy, and the ministry, which I have received of the Lord Jesus, to testify the gospel of the grace of God. To the church at Philippi Paul likens his life and death to the drink offering of the Old Testament. He literally "poured himself out." Paul is referring to the drink offering. This was a cup of wine that was poured out every morning and every evening on the burnt offering. It was never used for any other offering. Remember, the burnt offering is an Old Testament picture of salvation. From Exodus 29:38-41 we learn that the burnt offering included:

✡ The lamb of the first year without spot and blemish. This represents Jesus as the Lamb of God that taketh away the sin of the world.

✡ Flour mingled with oil. This represents Christ as the Bread of Life and the Holy Spirit resting both upon and in Him.

✡ Wine was poured out on the sacrifice. Wine is the symbol of joy in the Bible and also represents the blood of Jesus. Jesus emptied Himself of joy to become the Man of Sorrows. He poured out His life by pouring His blood. *Leviticus 17:11 For the life of the flesh is in the blood: and I have given it to you upon the altar to make an atonement for your souls: for it is the blood that maketh an atonement for the soul.* Allow me to remind you also of the fact that the blood of Jesus was not spilled but out poured. There is a difference. A spill is an accident. To pour is on purpose. The shedding of the blood of Jesus was no accident. It was not done by happenstance. It was a divine outpouring according to the will of His Father. *Hebrews 9:22 And almost all things are by the law purged with blood; and without shedding of blood is no remission.*

It was in the spirit of this sacrifice that he wrote to the church at Philippi. He said that he wanted "be offered" upon the altar of their sacrifice and faith. This word "be offered" is the Greek word *spendo*. Obviously, this is where we get our word "spend" from. Paul spent himself for the church. *2 Corinthians 12:15 And I will very gladly spend and be spent for you; though the more abundantly I love you, the less I be loved.* When the drink offering was poured upon the meat offering, it evaporated into steam. You never saw the drink offering on the sacrifice. You only saw the Lamb. Paul was saying that he was pouring out his life for the Lamb of God. His life was a vapor not to be seen, but only to be consumed in the life of Christ. This is the result of the surrendered life. Sad, but true, there are so few saved and fewer still that are wholly surrendered to God. I have heard it said that there are two great days in a Christian's life. The first great day is the day you get saved. The second great day in your life is the day in which you surrender your life wholly unto God. A life that is wholly yielded to God is a holy life indeed. To wholly give ourselves is the only way to truly be holy unto God.

It is, however, certain that before any servcie that we do for God or man is likely to be of lasting and permanent benefit, it must be saturated with our heart's blood. That which costs us nothing will not benefit others. If there is no expenditure of tears and prayer, if that love, of which the Apostle speaks in another place, which costs, is wanting, we may speak with the tongues of men and of angels, may know all mysteries and all knowledge, may bestow all our goods to feed the poor, but it will profit nothing. ~F.B. Meyer

May God give to His Church holy men who care nothing for personal gain and comfort but who are willing to follow the path of sacrifice for the achievement of its divinely-chosen goals. The mind of Christ is the model for the mind of the pastor. The passion of Christ is the pattern for every pastor. ~B.H. Carroll

Moses asked God to blot his name out of the book of life if God would not be merciful to His people. Jesus wept over Jerusalem and sent a Pentecost. Paul wished that he could be accursed for his brethren the Jews. These loved not their lives even unto death. The whole of the church of God ought to follow the example of our Savior and such godly examples. We are to pour our lives out and sacrifice ourselves for the salvation of the lost. To be poured out in death did not give Paul a heavy heart. Death was a reason to rejoice. Paul was rejoicing with the church, and he wanted the church at Philippi to rejoice with him at the time of his death as well. There is always a mourning for the loss of those we love, but Paul told the church at Thessalonica that as Christians, *we sorrow not as others which have no hope.* We may always rejoice when a child of God goes to be with Jesus. In Ecclesiastes 7:1, Solomon tells us that the day of our death is better than the day of our birth.

Timothy

Since Paul cannot come to Philippi himself, he sends Timothy in his place. There was no one closer to Paul than Timothy. Timothy was a native of either Derbe or Lystra- Acts 16:1. His mother, Eunice, was a Jew, and his grandmother was a lady named Lois. His father was a Greek- 2 Timothy 1:5. Timothy had most likely been educated in Greek customs to some extent because he was uncircumcised. His father seems to have faded off the scene. His mother and grandmother had been saved and were now raising him in a Christian home. Paul had found Timothy on his second missionary journey when he came to Lystra. From that time on it appears they were inseparable.

- ✝ Paul often called him his child in the Lord in countless Scriptures- 1 Corinthians 4:17; 1 Timothy 1:2.
- ✝ He was with Paul in Philippi- Acts 16.
- ✝ He was with Paul in Thessalonica and Berea- Acts 17:1-14.
- ✝ He was with Paul at Corinth and Ephesus- Acts 18:5, 19:21-22.
- ✝ He was with him in prison in Rome- Philippians 1:1; Colossians 1:1.

✝ He is connected with Paul in the writing of no less than six epistles- 1 & 2 Thessalonians, 2 Corinthians, Colossians, Philippians and Romans.

Dear Timothy! Paul had no one who was so likeminded! He was Timothy's spiritual father in the Lord. He had served with Paul in the gospel ministry. I am sure that Paul stood in the place of Timothy's earthly father as well. Paul loved Philippi so much that he parted with the one he loved dearest on this earth. He sent the very best he could send them. He could have sent Luke or even Epaphroditus alone, but he did not. Paul's love was so deep for the Philippians, and their need was so great, that he sent the one dearest and most like himself to stand in his stead. One of Timothy's many great qualities was that he was willing to go anywhere with any message for Paul. Timothy was sent with Paul's message, and Paul's message was always safe in Timothy's hands. Thank the Lord for those who come with good news from a far country.

In these verses we find that Paul sent Timothy to check on the state of the church. He sent Timothy to find out what kind of condition the church was in. Verse twenty-one is a sad commentary on the state of the church. Two thousand years later, the same can be found to be true of far too many churches. Murmurings and disputings are the result of every man seeking his own profit and not the things of Christ. Here we must refer ourselves back to the fourth verse of this chapter for the will of God concerning His church. Paul also admonished the members at Corinth to not seek their own profit. *1Corinthians 10:24 Let no man seek his own, but every man another's wealth.* He told them in chapter thirteen that charity...*Doth not behave itself unseemly, seeketh not her own, is not easily provoked, thinketh no evil.* In spite of all these holy instructions, self-seeking and self-glorying have only increased with the approaching of the coming day of Christ. The Scriptures are filled with holy and victorious examples and horrible villains of evil within the church. Consider the names of Diotrophes, Demas, Simon the Sorcerer, Hymenaeus, Alexander, and an unholy host of others. There have even been entire groups who have risen through evil in the church, just as the Nicolaitanes did. We derive our word "laity" or "layman" from this group. Even our word "clergy" comes from this group. They believe in "the rule of the people." They were those who were not pastors but rose to become "rulers of the people" by taking away the oversight of the pastor. They brought the church into bondage. In Revelation Jesus Himself declared His hatred of their deeds. God has never been democratic. God has no interest in the will or the rule of the people. Beloved brethren, we are more accountable to God than these. We have something nineteen centuries later that they did not have- a completed New Testament. We can know the mind and the will of God through His Word. That makes us more accountable.

Rest assured, that if you put Christ in the second place, and your own things first, you will hear of it at the Judgment Seat. ~Unknown

Timothy was a proven servant. Every servant of Christ should have such a testimony. Sir Henry Bartle Frere was a British officer who governed in India and Africa for many years. A man wrote this of him: "When Sir Bartle Frere returned from India, the carriage was sent to the village station to bring him to his home. When the new footman, but newly engaged, asked how he should recognize Sir Bartle, his aged mother said, 'Look out for somebody helping someone else.' Sure enough, when the London train had drawn in, the manservant observed a gentlemen assisting an old lady to the platform and then jumping back into the carriage to fetch out her luggage. Going straight to him, the footman enquired, 'Sir, Bartle?' Yes; it was he." Great would be the testimony of Christianity if all of God's people could have such a reputation. Not only was Timothy a proven servant, but he would also be a proven shepherd. Paul knew that no matter what the state of the church, Timothy could take good care of the church and lead them back to the state they needed to be in.

Epaphroditus

Paul hoped to be able to return to Philippi shortly. If you look at the chronology of Philippians and 1 Timothy 1:3 there is credibility given to the fact that Paul was released from prison and re-visited Philippi. If he was never able to return, Philippi would be well-cared for in the hands of Timothy and Epaphroditus.

Dear Epaphroditus! He is so easily passed by in our Bible study as we look at others more often mentioned. Let us not neglect him. Paul described Epaphroditus as his brother, companion in labour and fellow-soldier. This is high praise from the apostle to the Gentiles. It is most likely that this is also Epaphras mentioned by Paul in his epistle to the Colossians. *Colossians 4:12 Epaphras, who is one of you, a servant of Christ, saluteth you, always labouring fervently for you in prayers, that ye may stand perfect and complete in all the will of God.* Epaphroditus means "favored of Aphrodite." Aphrodite was the Greek goddess of love and beauty, who answered to the Roman goddess Venus. She was the wife of Zeus. Epaphroditus did not grow up in a Christian home. He grew up in a pagan home. Epaphras is a diminutive form of Epaphroditus, much like Douglas and Doug, Alan and Al, and so on. It is the same name, but the name of the Greek god is diminished. Epaphras simply means "favored" or "grace." Epaphroditus had been favored by God's grace and was gloriously saved. He no longer bare the name of a pagan God, but would eventually come to be known as a recipient of God's grace.

There is a great dramatic story in these verses that must not be lost. Remember that the Philippians had lost contact with Paul for ten years. When they had heard that he was in prison in Rome, they sent Epaphroditus with a financial gift. Along with that gift, Epaphroditus was sent to be a servant of Paul. Epaphroditus most likely volunteered, and the church was in agreement with his service. You see, anyone who offered himself to be the personal attendant of a man awaiting trial in the emperor's court, risked the death penalty himself by association. Epaphroditus put his life at risk to serve Paul.

While in Rome, Epaphroditus became sick and nearly died. Perhaps he fell ill with the Roman fever that so often swept through the city like a plague. He would not have had the immune system that others, who were indigenous to the area, would have had he being a foreigner. The word "sick" is the Greek word *astheneo*. It means to be weak or feeble. It is used seventeen times in the New Testament in reference to physical sickness. Three times it refers specifically to physical breakdowns of the body. The Christian must be careful that in his zeal and work for Christ we do not over exert the physical body God has given us. Work is not given to us so the body may be abused by being overworked. Our work does not enable us beyond what is the reasonable service of our body. When I first became a pastor, an older man of God came to speak in our church. He was in his late seventies then. He had been a pastor for years and also taught in Bible college. He was a great scholar on the authority of the Bible. He had written many things on the subject and gave them all to me. I asked him what council he would give to me as an older preacher to a younger one. I was twenty-nine or thirty at the time. Tears began to stream down his cheeks and he said to me, "Get a good night's rest." He told me that for years he would go about his church work in the day and then stay up long into the night reading, writing and studying. He slept very little. He said that now he was an old man whose body wanted and needed rest, but he could not sleep because he trained his body not to rest for all those years. I took heed to his counsel. There will always be something left undone. Even God rested one day in seven to teach man that rest refreshes us in the work and lengthens our work. There must be a persistence that says Christ may come today, but there must also be a patience that sustains us. We need fervency and urgency, but rest replenishes our energy.

There are those who teach that if a Christian gets sick that it is a mark of sin in our life. Of course, this is completely untrue, and this passage is evidence to that fact. Sickness can come from God as much as good health. Paul never taught the false doctrine of "healing in the atonement" as the birthright of believers. Paul had an apostolic "sign gift" of healing, but we never read of Paul nor any of his close fellow-laborers being healed. Paul still had his thorn in the flesh. *2 Corinthians 12:7 And lest I should be exalted above measure through the abundance of the revelations, there was given to me a thorn in the flesh, the messenger of Satan to buffet me, lest I should be exalted above measure.* God had to keep Paul physically weak in order to continue to give him spiritual strength for which God alone could be credited. Timothy had to take a little wine for his stomach's sake. Paul had to leave Trophimus in Miletus because he was too sick to travel. By this time, much New Testament Scripture had been written and scattered abroad to the churches, and the record of miraculous healings had passed off the scene. To be sure, God should be given the praise for every prayer that is answered by healing, but Paul said that the healing of God on Epaphroditus was an act of God's mercy not a miracle. Mercy is a greater honor than a physical miracle. Mercy endures forever.

As much as Epaphroditus loved Paul and loved serving him, he still had a longing for his church back home. Epaphroditus was burdened by the concern the church back home had for him. The words "full of heaviness" is the Greek word *adamoneo.* It also means "heavily burdened." He was burdened for his home church when he heard of their sympathy for his sickness. Epaphroditus was so compassionate that he felt bad when others were feeling sorry for him. It seems that he was not as concerned about the sickness that nearly took his life as much as he cared for those who were concerned for him.

Paul referred to Epaphroditus as Philippi's messenger. The word messenger is the word *apostolos.* It is the same word as "apostle." An apostle is simple a "sent one" or "one sent on an errand." By using this word, Paul places Epaphroditus in the ranks of the apostles. By definition, God sends us all on His heavenly errand with His heavenly message- the Gospel. There are those who falsely claim they are apostles today. They are claiming the authority and the power of the twelve that were ordained by God in an unusual way to propagate the Gospel as the Scriptures were completed. Our power and authority today is found in Bible, yet we are all still supposed to be "sent ones." *John 20:21 Then said Jesus to them again, Peace be unto you: as my Father hath sent me, even so send I you.* This verse was given to the apostles in the upper room, yet we all rightfully claim it as a Great Commission verse. Jesus has committed unto us His Gospel and He sends us even as He was sent by His Father.

The word Paul uses for minister here is the Greek word *leitourgos*. In the cities of ancient Greece, there were men who, because of love for their city, would at their own expense undertake certain civic duties. Out of their own pockets they would pay the costs of delegations, some drama of the poets, or even the training of athletes who would represent their city at the Grecian games. They might pay for the fitting out of a ship of war or pay a crew to serve in the state's naval forces. These *leitourgos* were the supreme benefactors of their city.

Paul takes the Christian word *apostolos* and the Greek word *leitourgos* and applies them both to Epaphroditus. In essence Paul says, "Give such a man a welcome home. Honor him for he risked his life for Christ." This was a very important message for he was sent to serve and returning home could be perceived as quitting or cowardice. He was not a coward, nor a quitter. Paul needed him more in Philippi than he did in Rome. He had to make sure to send him home with high honors. How thoughtful for a man whose own life was in peril before Nero. This is classic Paul. He always considered the needs of others before his own.

I am glad that there has always been a Timothy or an Epaphroditus who are ready and willing to go wherever God sends them, whenever God sends them. They remind us of the prophet Isaiah. *Isaiah 6:8 Also I heard the voice of the Lord, saying, Whom shall I send, and who will go for us? Then said I, Here am I; send me.* We need such ready and willing servants. When I was in the service I was part of a group that was designated as "world-wide deployable." Many but not all in the service have this designation. It meant that they can be anywhere in the world they are needed within twenty-four hours. We were always ready, always on standby. Heaven's host needs such soldiers as well. We may go far or not so far. Consider the apostle Andrew. He is little spoken of among the apostles, but he went far enough to bring his brother, Peter, to Jesus. Peter preached, and three thousand were saved at Pentecost. One preacher said that Andrew's fruit from that day would be three thousand and one because without an Andrew, there might not be a Peter. Eight days later another five thousand were saved on the last day of the feast. All this and more because one man introduced his brother to Jesus. Heaven crowns those who will go where God sends them.

Men like Epaphroditus are to be received gladly and held in high reputation. We do not put people on pedestals for the pedestal might tip and the image break, but we do look to those in high reputation and hold them dear to our hearts. How do we determine who is worthy of high reputation? High reputation is not given because of intellectual wisdom, social standing, wealth, musical talent, acting or athletic ability. It is reserved for those who labor in the work of Christ. We have the wrong heroes today. I often tell our church that we need to tear down the posters of the heroes of this world from the walls our children's bedrooms and replace them with the prayer cards of our missionaries. They are the true heroes. Jeremiah said that he would get to the great men for they have known the way of the Lord. We need to hold in high esteem great servants of God. We need to revive the names of great servants of Christ. Epaphroditus has had many fellow laborers in Christ- James Black, Daisy Hawes, Edward Kimble, H.G. Spafford and countless others. Heroes, such as Timothy have been found in the pulpit for centuries through the voices of men like, Charles Spurgeon, Joseph Parker, Henry Ironside, George Truett, J. Frank Norris, Jack Hyles and countless others. They have been found on the mission field with Paul like the ranks of William Carey, Hudson Taylor, Adoniram Judson, David Livingstone, C.T. Studd, Bill Borden, John Paton, Andrew Murray and another vast host. We need to hold in high esteem on earth those who are held in high esteem in heaven. These folks, like Epaphroditus, did not regard their life. These did whatever had to be done in order to fully serve the church God sent them to. Nothing was found lacking in what they supplied to the church. Does your church lack because you have not brought the full supply God has given you? Let us be offered as Paul and pour out lives as living sacrifices holy, acceptable unto God, which is our reasonable service.

Chapter 3

Rejoicing In Christ Our Prize

In chapter 3 Paul reminds the church at Philippi to continue towards their heavenly prize. There would be those that would come and try to derail the church from within. They would bring doctrinal and personality conflicts within the church. The church would need to remain steadfast and focused on their goal. He also gives a solemn admonition to have no confidence in the flesh- neither our own nor anyone else's. This is a necessary warning, as it is the nature of humanity to regard our own righteousness and morality. We will certainly fall short in life if we are leaning on the arm of our flesh.

Paul's Persistent Precaution- Philippians 3:1-3

Philippians 3:1-3 *Finally, my brethren, rejoice in the Lord. To write the same things to you, to me indeed is not grievous, but for you it is safe. Beware of dogs, beware of evil workers, beware of the concision. For we are the circumcision, which worship God in the spirit, and rejoice in Christ Jesus, and have no confidence in the flesh.*

Finally.... Paul does not use this word casually like a preacher who is trying to close his sermon with four more points. Some are quick to point out that Paul also says finally in Philippians 4:8. There is a difference. Finally means "as for the rest" or "the things that remain." In chapter 3 Paul uses the word finally as "for the rest" in regards to himself. In chapter 4 he uses finally as "for the rest" of those things regarding the church at Philippi. Paul has caused us to rejoice in Christ our position (chapter one) and Christ our paradigm (Chapter two). As for the rest (chapter three), he rejoices because Christ is his prize- verse fourteen. Paul said that all that remains for him is to rejoice in the Lord. The last thing Paul did was rejoice in the Lord. I believe that Paul rejoiced in Jesus as he bent down to lay his head on the chopping block. He exhorts the church at Philippi (and churches today as well) to rejoice in the Lord. Joy that is found in Christ is indestructible joy. It is eternal joy. It rejoices in Christ and not circumstance. It is based on the fact that a Christian lives eternally in the presence of Jesus. A Christian may lose all they hold dear- everyone and everything- but they can never lose Jesus. Joy should be natural to the spiritual man. It is part of the fruit that the Holy Spirit bears in our lives. Joy is not for the natural man. He can have earthly happiness. He can have temporary pleasure when something good "happens." After all, God causes it to rain on both the just and the unjust, but happiness is temporal and when the moment passes so does the pleasure. The natural man might experience earthly joy in the things God has given all men. The Bible tells us that God has given us all things richly to enjoy. The Bible speaks of the joy when a child is born. Again, the joy is done when the life is done if that soul steps out into a Christless eternity. So we see that there is earthly joy and eternal joy. Eternal joy is one of those things that comes from God and is given only to God's people. Jesus spent His final evening with the disciples, and one of the things He spoke to them of was His joy. *John 15:11 These things have I spoken unto you, that my joy might remain in you, and that your joy might be full.* This was to be a bittersweet evening. There was sorrow mingled with joy, but there was joy in the presence of Jesus. Joy does not leave when sorrow comes. The joy of Jesus is our peace and our comfort in the midst of our sorrows. The cross was before Jesus, but joy was beyond Him. *Hebrews 12:2 Looking unto Jesus the author and finisher of our faith; who for the joy that was set before him endured the cross, despising the shame, and is set down at the right hand of the throne of God.* The children of Israel were in terrible circumstances when Nehemiah told them to rejoice. *Nehemiah 8:10 Then he said unto them, Go your way, eat the fat, and drink the sweet, and send portions unto them for whom nothing is prepared: for this day is holy unto our Lord: neither be ye sorry; for the joy of the LORD is your strength.* King David reminds us that our joy is not dictated by circumstance, environment or abundance. *Psalms 16:11 Thou wilt shew me the path of life: in thy presence is fulness of joy; at thy right hand there are pleasures for evermore.* Joy is based on knowing Jesus. If you know Jesus, you can rejoice and sing with Paul in his prison cell. *John 17:13 And now come I to thee; and these things I speak in the world, that they might have my joy fulfilled in themselves.* This is not a command to express simple words. It is a reality of Christian experience. It is sad to see Christians, who have every reason to rejoice, act like complainers, crips and cranks. It is a poor testimony that many that are lost have little or no desire to know our Savior because they do not see His joy in our lives. Margaret Fuller wrote in her diary of Ralph Waldo Emerson (a Christian man with a Christian testimony), "Emerson came into our house this morning with a sunbeam on his face." If we would live in the Spirit, the joy of Jesus will be a natural product in our life.

We may not be able to rejoice in our circumstances, friends, or prospects, but we can always rejoice in Jesus Christ, whose Nature is the key to the understanding and unlocking of all mysteries, the Well-spring of hope, the Day-star in our hearts, till 'the morning breaks and the shadows flee away.' ~F.B. Meyer

Notice what Paul now says...*To write the same things is not grievous...*this implies that Paul had probably written letters to the Philippians before which have not survived. He was writing to them again of things he had written to them before. Paul wrote epistles (letters) for sixteen years (AD 48-64). Certainly he wrote more than fourteen letters in those sixteen years. Repeating this message was not a tiresome task for Paul, and it was not a vain repetition for the saints. He was doing as he so often had done, He was stirring up the church in order to put them in remembrance. Anything worth saying

146

once is worth repeating. There is no harm in hearing old truths again and again. We think nothing of eating the same foods and drinking the same water every day. We think nothing of getting up at the same time and doing the same work. It should be nothing for us to hear once again things we have heard before. I was taught all through my youth that repetition is the key to memorization and memorization is the key to learning. Paul did not want them to ever forget to rejoice in the Lord. Perhaps this is why the word is found so many times in these four short chapters.

Paul tells us to "beware" three times in verse two. He tells us to beware of dogs, evil workers and the concision. Paul was speaking of the Judaizers when he spoke of dogs and evil workers. He is describing the two ways in which they infiltrate the church. One way they attack is openly aggressive. The other way is extremely deceitful. The final "beware" is against those that cover their darkness with light. The Judaizers were that group of people that claimed you first had to become a full Jew before you could become a complete Christian. They wanted to mix Judaism and Christianity into one religious belief system. Among other things, they claimed a man had to be circumcised before he could be saved. They truly were legalists in that they added their works to the finished work of Christ.

Beware of dogs

The dogs Paul speaks of here are not our well-loved domesticated pets. They are not the well-loved beautiful breeds that we know today.

These are the pye-dogs of the middle east. In the middle east and many other poor countries, dogs run wild in the city and the countryside. They are vicious scavengers, running in wild packs without homes or owners. They go through the garbage dumps and snarl at all who come close to them. They are very flighty and skittish when approached individually. They even bite and devour among themselves, which is the specific reference Paul is making to the church at Philippi.

There were going to be groups of the Judaizers that would come in and very aggressively try to bite and devour in the church. Paul warned the churches of Galatia of this internal destruction as well. *Galatians 5:15 But if ye bite and devour one another, take heed that ye be not consumed one of another.* I was hunting hogs in Texas several years ago. A friend and I were in a very remote area. When we turned off the paved road, we drove for thirty minutes over rock and water to get to a simple cabin with no water or electricity. We killed our first hog and gutted it just about thirty feet from the cabin. We figured there were coyotes and bobcats in the area. We did not know about the packs of wild dogs. That night a pack of wild dogs came in to the place where we had butchered the hog. I am very accustomed to the woods, the dark and wild animals, but I have never heard noise like that in my life. We had shotguns, pistols, rifles and bows. We were in a cabin with four walls. We should have felt safe, but we stayed up all night with shotguns in hand watching the door.

Dogs are the lowest of the low in the Scriptures. David told Saul that he was not worth Saul's pursuits. It was like chasing a dead dog because David had never been the source of any harm to Saul. Jesus said not to give that which is holy to the dogs. In the book of Revelation the dog stands for those who are so impure that they are banned from the Holy City. In the book of Deuteronomy the Law likened the price of a dog to the hire of a whore. Pagan temples always had houses joined to the side of them where men and women prostituted themselves as acts of worship to their false gods. Immorality always comes with idolatry. The price of a dog was the price of the sodomite. It was the lowest form of an act of worship to a pagan god. In 2 Kings 23 King Josiah broke down the houses of the sodomites that had been physically attached to the temple. He also took down the grove with all the hangings that the women had made as they worshipped heathen gods in the temple of the one true God. There are always going to be dogs who come prostituting perversion in the house of the Lord.

It appears that Paul was making reference to the words which God had spoken through the prophet Isaiah. *Isaiah 56:10-11 His watchmen are blind: they are all ignorant, they are all dumb dogs, they cannot bark; sleeping, lying down, loving to slumber. Yea, they are greedy dogs which can never have enough, and they are shepherds that cannot understand: they all look to their own way, every one for his gain, from his quarter.* Isaiah warned against false prophets who were attempting to comfort the people when the truth was they were under impending judgment. They were telling them that everything was all right instead of warning them of the coming bondage. To be dumb is to have lost the power to speak. These false prophets were dumb dogs. They would not say anything. There are no shortage of pastors who refuse to speak out today and call sin by name. Sin is at best a broad general term dealt with in a broad and general fashion with no clear message of repentance, restitution and reconciliation. I have often said that you might go to one church and never have a problem with what is said. It is what you will never hear that is the problem. Comfort, convenience and tolerance are the words of today. God is the God of all our present grace, but we never hear of His coming judgment. Judgment is mentioned over a hundred times more than grace in the Bible. We need preaching on grace, but we must not neglect judgment either. I know more than one man whose God is a God of grace without judgment. Half a God is no God at all.

A good sheep dog is always looking and listening for danger. If he smells or sees a lion, bear or a wolf, he will bark. He might see movement and cannot tell what it is but he is alert to the danger- kind of like a pastor today that will warn you about sin in a specific way. A good sheep dog will bark like a maniac and try to scare the danger away. Jesus echoes Isaiah in the Sermon on the Mount. *Matthew 7:6 Give not that which is holy unto the dogs, neither cast ye your pearls before swine, lest they trample them under their feet, and turn again and rend you.* Jesus tells us not to try and persuade these dumb dogs. They do not want the truth. They do not desire holiness. They only

150

desire personal gain with minimal effort. You cannot offer the riches of truth and holiness to these people because their life is not based on right but on personal gain. You cannot argue with them. Paul knew that sooner or later the legalistic Judaizers would find their way to Philippi. These were the ones who prophetically were responsible for the crucifixion of Christ. *Psalms 22:16 For dogs have compassed me: the assembly of the wicked have inclosed me: they pierced my hands and my feet.* Paul said do not answer or argue with them, and do not give them the time of day.

Beware of evil workers

There is a difference between evil workers and evil doers. An evil doer seeks his own destruction. An evil worker seeks the destruction of others. F.B. Meyer called Paul's evil workers the "cranks of our churches." To be sure, I have not known a church that did not have cranks. There is also a difference between a dog and an evil worker. Dogs attack very aggressively. The evil workers come in and do their work very subtly. They will come in and pretend to be exactly like the rest of the church. They will win the hearts and the affections of the people. Once they have the hearts of the people, they promote their evil work and turn many astray. It is easy to find examples in the Bible. Absalom would be an evil worker. He stole the hearts of the men of Israel subtly. Adonijah would be like a dog, who very boldly set himself up in the Bible. Jesus spoke of the evil worker in his Sermon on the Mount. *Matthew 7:15 Beware of false prophets, which come to you in* sheep's clothing, but inwardly they are ravening wolves. Evil workers draw people farther away from God under the pretense of bringing them closer to God.

Beware of the Concision

There were not many Jews in Philippi and there were even fewer Jewish Christians, yet the Judaizers always seemed to come following after Paul in an attempt to destroy all the good the Gospel had done. That is true today. In the Greek there are two verbs which are very much alike. There is the verb *peritemnein* which means "to circumcise," and there is the verb *katatemnein* which means "mutilate." The word concision is the word for mutilation. The word circumcision is the verb for circumcision's cutting away. One is a sacred rite, and the other an act of mutilation.

You see the Judaizers professed true circumcision, but Paul accused them of being mutilators, while professing that Christianity was the true circumcision. *Romans 2:26-29 Therefore if the uncircumcision keep the righteousness of the law, shall not his uncircumcision be counted for circumcision? And shall not uncircumcision which is by nature, if it fulfil the law, judge thee, who by the letter and circumcision dost transgress the law? For he is not a Jew, which is one outwardly; neither is that circumcision, which is outward in the flesh: But he is a Jew, which is one inwardly; and circumcision is that of the heart, in the spirit, and not in the letter; whose praise is not of men, but of God.* The Judaizers did not deny that Jesus was the Messiah or that His Gospel was the power of God unto salvation. They did, however, insist that the Gentiles be circumcised. They claimed that Gentiles could not come to the fullness of the Gospel without coming through the Law of Moses. They were the legalists of their day. They claimed you had to become a Jew first by circumcision before Christ could save through the blood of His cross. The Bible records that there was a council in Acts 15 over the circumcision of the Gentiles of Galatia. The Scripture clearly records that circumcision has nothing to do with our salvation. *Galatians 6:15 For in Christ Jesus neither circumcision availeth any thing, nor uncircumcision, but a new creature.* The old circumcision is out. It is not just an external observance. True New Testament circumcision is done in the heart. The old circumcision was a sign of the flesh. The new is a sign of the work of faith wrought in our heart. The physical circumcision was a sign to teach of inward circumcision. *Deuteronomy 10:16 Circumcise therefore the foreskin of your heart, and be no more stiffnecked.* God said that He would circumcise the hearts of Israel to cause His people to truly love Him as they should. *Deuteronomy 30:6 And the LORD thy God will circumcise thine heart, and the heart of thy seed, to love the LORD thy God with all thine heart, and with all thy soul, that thou mayest live.* Paul was saying that if all you have to show for your faith is circumcision in the flesh, you are not really circumcised at all.

We are not short of Judaizers today. They come in different shades and colors of denominational heresies. They claim that in order to be saved you have to be baptized, hold membership in a certain church, keep sacraments or be filled with the Spirit in a way that the Spirit has never filled anyone. They might require us to pass through the confessional, pay indulgences, hold to certain fasts, abstain from marriage, or perform grievous acts of self-denial. Salvation is Jesus Christ plus nothing, minus nothing. Paul was saying, "beware of those who make you pass through ceremony for salvation."

Paul tells us in verse three that Christians are truly the circumcision of Christ today if they will do three things:

1. Worship God in the spirit.
2. Rejoice in Christ Jesus.
3. Have no confidence in the flesh.

Those who meet this criteria will show that they are the true descendants of Abraham today. These are Abraham's seed who have been grafted in. *Galatians 3:7 Know ye therefore that they which are of faith, the same are the children of Abraham.*

First, we are to worship God in the spirit. The word spirit has a small "s." This refers to the spirit of man. We are to bring our spirit in line with the Spirit of God. *John 4:23 But the hour cometh, and now is, when the true worshippers shall worship the Father in spirit and in truth: for the Father seeketh such to worship him.* What many call worship today is nothing but sensual. Worship is not vain tradition or ritual like Paul's day. It is not the sensationalism or emotionalism we see today. It is worshipping God with all our heart. It is a right attitude

154

and a right approach to God. We should come to God's house with a heart to know and please God and not simply appease a religious conscience or some selfish desire of the flesh. We should come to gain more knowledge of Jesus so that we will have a better relationship and offer better service. Worship always involved humility and sacrifice in the Bible. The first time we find the word "worship" in the Bible, we find Abraham offering to God that which he held dearest to his heart-his son Isaac. The truth is that most people are not interested in true Biblical worship because they believe that worship means getting something from God, as opposed to what it really is, giving to God. The offering is the one tangible act of worship in our services. It is the time when we give or offer unto God a sacrifice of faith and obedience from our heart through our daily labors.

Second, we are to rejoice in Christ. Once again the prevailing theme and admonition is to rejoice in our Christ. Paul immediately brings us back to verse one after warning us in verse two. Rejoice in Christ no matter what. This is the true mark of circumcision of the heart. Finally, make sure the first and last thing you do is to rejoice in Jesus.

Third, we are told to have no confidence in the flesh. The best of men are men at best. Even great men have great flaws. Paul reminds us in Romans 7 that in our flesh dwells no good thing. There is nothing good about the flesh, and yet there is nothing that is not good about Christ. Christians that rejoice in Christ, boast in Christ and not themselves. Anything good done in our life is not according to what

155

we have done for ourselves but what Christ has done for us. I have heard pastors say that anything that goes right in the church is a blessing of the Lord and anything that is wrong is their fault. They are boasting in the Lord and giving neither confidence nor credit to the flesh. The flesh can never improve, and the new nature can never be improved upon. *Romans 8:7 Because the carnal mind is enmity against God: for it is not subject to the law of God, neither indeed can be.* The spiritual mind is the mind of Christ. If we walk in the Spirit we will not fulfill the lusts of the flesh; however, we are never safe from our flesh. Walking in the Spirit does not remove the desire of the flesh. Even after years of godly living, the flesh is still present to do evil. You can have your best year of church attendance, Bible reading, time in prayer and witnessing, and yet the flesh will be still there patiently waiting for a moment of apathy to lead you into a great fall. David was forty years of age, a seasoned man of God and King, when he committed adultery with Bathsheba. He went another thirty years carefully guarding his flesh, and then once again he sinned by numbering the people. Do not let your years cause you to let your guard down. The flesh has been present for thousand of years, and we are here for less than a hundred. Your flesh is no better at the end of your Christian life than it was at the very beginning.

Paul's Past Pedigree- Philippians 3:4-6

Philippians 3:4-6 *Though I might also have confidence in the flesh. If any other man thinketh that he hath whereof he might trust in the flesh,*

I more: Circumcised the eighth day, of the stock of Israel, of the tribe of Benjamin, an Hebrew of the Hebrews; as touching the law, a Pharisee; Concerning zeal, persecuting the church; touching the righteousness which is in the law, blameless.

Here in these verses Paul is going to give his past pedigree in order to show that if salvation was to be earned, he had more right to boast than all his adversaries. He will then show how that all he has boasted in counts for nothing but loss to obtain salvation. Salvation is of the Lord and through Christ alone.

The Jews claimed authority over this apostle's doctrine because they were Jews. It is almost as if they are saying, "Paul, what do you know about Judaism and the Law? You are a Christian." Paul reminds them that he was more Jewish in his past, than these accusers were in their present. The truth is they were not half the Jew that Paul had been. He will give an autobiography and substantiate his claim that he is more than all his critics. Paul was willing to stack his life as a Jew up against any other Jew. Paul could say as no other, *"I more."* He knew what it meant to be a Jew in the highest sense. He deliberately gave it all up for Christ. We have already seen in chapter two the seven steps of both our Savior's humility and exaltation. Here we find Paul's seven steps of religious self-righteousness:

1. Circumcised the eighth day.
2. Of the stock of Israel.
3. Of the tribe of Benjamin.

4. An Hebrew of the Hebrews.

5. As touching the law, a Pharisee.

6. Zealous as persecuting the church.

7. Blameless in the law.

Paul was circumcised the eighth day- Genesis 17:9, 25; Leviticus 12:1-3. Paul was not a Gentile proselyte that had entered Judaism. He was born into Judaism and from the very beginning his life was devoted to Judaism. His parents saw to it that he was circumcised according to the Law on the eighth day. This was the duty of all good Jewish families. John the Baptist- Luke 1:59-and Jesus- Luke 2:21 were circumcised on the eighth day. Paul was circumcised and notably on the eighth day. Circumcision was not just a Jewish custom. The Ishmaelites were all circumcised; however, they circumcise in the thirteenth year as opposed to the eighth day. They were circumcised at thirteen because that was the age when Ishmael was circumcised. Paul's circumcision was lawful not simply ancestral. Since Calvary, true circumcision is no longer found as an ordinance of the flesh but of the heart. It is the putting off of the old man and the putting on of the new. We put off sin and put on righteousness.

Paul was of the stock of Israel- Genesis 29:21-30:25; 35:16-29. When a Jew really wanted to stress their divine heritage they laid claim to Israel. Many were of the seed of Abraham. God promised that Abraham would be the father of many nations. Ishmael was of the seed of Abraham and so were his twelve sons, who were known as dukes and princes. Edom and his seed were of the seed of Abraham through Isaac. Only an Israelite could trace his seed to Abraham through Jacob and his twelve sons as the purest stock of God's chosen people.

Paul was of the tribe of Benjamin. Of the twelve sons of Jacob, Benjamin was a standout tribe. Many argue that Benjamin was the greatest tribe for several reasons. Jacob called his youngest son Benjamin, which means "the son of my right hand." Benjamin was the son of the right hand of Israel above all other sons. He was Jacob's walking stick, the one on whom he leaned. Remember, Joseph was taken from his father for seventeen years. During that time, the privilege of the favored son rested on Benjamin. Of the twelve sons of Jacob, Benjamin was the only son to actually be born in the land of promise- Genesis 35:17-18. Benjamin was the son of Rachel, Jacob's favorite wife. God's first choice for a king over Israel came through the seed of Benjamin- 1 Samuel 9:1-2. It is highly probable that Paul (Saul of Tarsus) was named after this king. When the kingdom of Israel was divided between Jeroboam and Rehoboam, Benjamin alone remained faithful to the grandson of King David when the rest of the nation was in rebellion- 1 Kings 12:21. This was no light thing. We expect Judah to be loyal. Rehoboam was their blood. Benjamin chose to remain with a king who had promised them a hard life in place of a king who promised ease. They chose the right thing in place of the easy thing. Benjamin had the honor of being first in battle when the nation went to war- Judges 5:13; Hosea 5:8. When the people returned from

Babylonian bondage, the tribes of Benjamin and Judah formed the nucleus of the returning remnant- Ezra 4:1. We would not have the story of Esther and the great deliverance of the Jews without Benjamin. Mordecai and Esther were both Benjamites. Paul's pedigree in Benjamin placed him in the aristocracy of Israel. It would be like someone in England whose genealogy came down through the Normans. It would be as an American who claimed direct lineage from the Pilgrim fathers who came over on the Mayflower.

Paul was an Hebrew of the Hebrews. Though he was raised in Tarsus, there was no Gentile blood in Paul's veins. He was not as the Samaritans and others who had mingled their blood with Syria, Babylon, Greece, Rome and other nations. He was a Hebrew of Hebrews alone. In his blood was only the blood of Abraham, the friend of God, who crossed the Euphrates and settled in Canaan land. This declaration also carries with it both a cultural and a linguistic claim. He was not a Hellenistic Jew. He had not adopted the language and customs of the Greeks. The Jews had assimilated in countless nations. There were tens of thousands of Jews in Rome. There were more than a million in Alexandria, Egypt alone. Many of them could not even speak the Hebrew language. Pentecost points this out in Acts 2. The Jews were often diligent to keep their blood lines clear and even faithful to culture and observance of the Law, but it was often a downfall that in their assimilation, they would not perpetuate the language of the Hebrews. A Hebrew of the Hebrews did not just define blood but also culture. Paul knew the Hebrew language- Acts 21:40.

Paul said that as touching the law he was a Pharisee. It was not always a bad thing to be a Pharisee. Paul used his claim as a Pharisee on more than one occasion- Acts 22:3; 23:6; 26:5; Philippians 3:5. There was a time when they were the best to be found among God's people. Today we look on a Pharisee as one full of pride and arrogance. We imagine one who looks good on the outside, but on the inside they are full of corruption. We look on them with scorn and contempt. However, if you were to go back to the time that lies silent between the pages of the Old and New Testaments, you will find them to be the vanguards of God's Law and the Temple. Jesus made a point using the Pharisees to stress practical righteousness during His Sermon on the Mount. *Matthew 5:20 For I say unto you, That except your righteousness shall exceed the righteousness of the scribes and Pharisees, ye shall in no case enter into the kingdom of heaven.* They were the true worshippers in a time of indifference and neglect. The name Pharisee means "Separated Ones." They separated themselves from all that was common in life in order to devote themselves wholly to the Law. They opposed the Herodians and the Sadducees. Yes, they built the tombs of the prophets. That was done initially because they had respect for their sacred past. Yes, they made broad their phylacteries. They wanted to stand out and be counted. They were not ashamed of the God that so many had swept out of their lives. The Pharisees were those who were most zealous over the moral, civil and ceremonial laws of Israel. There were not very many of them- never

161

more than six thousand amongst the six million Jews of Paul's day. Paul was of the very straitest sect of the Pharisees- Acts 26:5.

Paul was zealous as persecuting the church. Religious zeal is one of the highest qualities in life. Phinehas, the son of Aaron, was zealous for the Lord his God and put sin away from the camp of Israel. God told Phinehas that because of his zeal his seed would always have a place of service in the priesthood- Numbers 25:11-13. God promised him an everlasting priesthood. Paul had a zeal that was unmatched. Many hated the Christians, but it was Paul who was so devoted to Judaism that he did something to try and quench the light of Christianity. In his ignorance, Paul was trying to put Christianity away from the camp of Israel as Phinehas did. He breathed fire and used the sword like a tornado, attempting to snuff out the disciples of Christ. That was no small thing for any man, let alone a very young Saul of Tarsus.

Paul was blameless in the Law. Paul was not claiming that he had not committed any sin. His claim was one that signified that he had not neglected any part of the Law. The word blameless here comes from a Greek verb that means *to blame for sins of omission.* Paul did not omit any part of the Law- specifically the ceremonial part of the Law. That was the tradition the Pharisees valued most. It was the most public and the most tangible. He was considered clean by the keeping the sacrifices and feasts without fail. As a Pharisee, he paid close attention to every jot and every tittle. He left nothing out. He kept the whole Law. Everything the Law demanded, Paul fulfilled.

These former glories of Paul were useless to his position in Christ but powerful in his position to argue with the Jews. Paul proved to these Jews that he had the knowledge and the right to speak concerning both Christ and the Law. He was not an outside critic of Judaism, but a former partaker in the deepest sense and the utmost fulfillment.

Paul's Present Perspective- Philippians 3:7-9

Philippians 3:7-9 *But what things were gain to me, those I counted loss for Christ. Yea doubtless, and I count all things but loss for the excellency of the knowledge of Christ Jesus my Lord: for whom I have suffered the loss of all things, and do count them but dung, that I may win Christ, And be found in him, not having mine own righteousness, which is of the law, but that which is through the faith of Christ, the righteousness which is of God by faith:*

I love these verses. They are some of the sweetest words of testimony ever to be uttered that spoke of a man's love for his God. It would be wonderful indeed if every Christian could honestly speak these words from their heart as Paul.

Dr. B.H. Carroll once said, "When I was converted, I lost my religion." He was echoing the spirit of Paul's words here in verse seven. When a man's life has been transformed from one extreme to the other, that man takes on a new perspective. He evaluates what his life was and what it has become. All that Paul held dear in his old life was counted loss for Christ's sake and never was a man so happy to lose. I have known many who would never accept Jesus Christ because they were too much in love with their present life. When Paul met Jesus on the road to Damascus, he was never the same. Nothing else nor no one else would ever be worth living for compared to the bright light he saw on the road to Damascus that day. I do not believe there was ever a single moment in Paul's life where he would have traded back his new life for his old life and risk losing Christ. In this verse he reaffirms the faith that he has followed for nearly thirty years.

Paul stacked up all his righteousness on one side and Jesus on the other. As a Jew, his righteous works were his credits, and he counted Christ a debit. When he was converted, all changed. His righteousness were debts, and Christ was his credit for eternal life. His whole book keeping system was turned upside down. He was transformed from an accountant of self-righteousness to a steward of Jesus Christ. Paul walked away from all his advantages and privileges. He forfeited the respect of the Jews. Some folks have been misled to believe that God wants them to simply change religions. The truth is God wants us to forsake vain religion to come into a personal relationship with Jesus Christ. Paul was converted because he had a real experience with a real person- Jesus Christ- crucified, glorified and coming again.

Paul was not simply exchanging one religion for another; it was not one system of rites and ceremonies giving place to a superior system; or one set of doctrines, rules and regulations making way for a better one. He had come into actual contact with a divine Person, the once crucified, but now glorified Christ of God. ~Dr. Henry Ironside

The word "loss" used here is the Greek word *zemia*. It speaks of a loss applied to a trade. This word would be used by ships captains who voluntarily incurred a loss by casting their cargo over the side of their ship in some great storm. They would lighten the ship in order to survive the storm. Surviving the storm meant the loss of treasure in order to spare life. Life is the great treasure, and storms often prove it. This is exactly what Jesus taught in the gospels. *Matthew 16:25 For whosoever will save his life shall lose it: and whosoever will lose his life for my sake shall find it.* All those things that Paul had held to his credit before he was saved would never be counted for any good with God. God does not look on a man's work as good until that man has come to God through the finished work of Christ. The work of Christ in us is what gives value to our works before God. You see, before we are saved, we are working our own works our own way. Even though some of Paul's "things" or works were actually good works in and of themselves, they were never good enough to save.

*We cannot cling to the old life and make the new life count for Him.
A good thing becomes a bad thing if it keeps out the best thing. ~Dr.
Lehman Strauss*

When we are born again, we work the works that God has chosen
for us. *Ephesians 2:8-10 For by grace are ye saved through faith; and
that not of yourselves: it is the gift of God: Not of works, lest any man
should boast. For we are his workmanship, created in Christ Jesus unto
good works, which God hath before ordained that we should walk in
them.* These verses give us the proper progression. First is salvation
by grace through faith not of works. Then there is works ordained by
God because of our salvation. This is exactly as our Savior did also. He
worked only the works of the Father. *John 9:4 I must work the works
of him that sent me, while it is day: the night cometh, when no man can
work.*

It should be remembered that there are many years that have
passed for Paul between verses seven and eight. It had been a long
time since Paul had counted his righteousness as gain. To know Jesus
was Paul's passionate pursuit.   He stripped himself of all his
righteousness and personal achievement to know Jesus.

There is more than one kind of knowledge of Jesus. Many know
about Jesus. They know that He is God's Son. They know He died on
the cross. They know He shed His blood and was resurrected. They
know facts, but they have not personally accepted those facts by faith
from the heart. They have head knowledge of Jesus but not the

166

personal relationship that is begun at salvation by faith from the heart. Paul knew Jesus personally. That is knowledge that excels far beyond knowing about Jesus. Paul had a personal relationship with Jesus Christ. When young people get married, they think they know the person they love. It does not take long at all to figure out they never really knew the one they loved like they thought they did. Through the years their knowledge grows and so does their love for each other. This is why husbands are told to dwell with their wives according to knowledge. It is sad that many share a mortgage responsibility but never a marriage relationship. I knew a pastor who was going through some trouble in his ministry. Trouble always brings out the real person. He told me that he and his wife had been married for more than ten years and he said that he felt like he did not even know her. Paul really knew Jesus. He could look back on years of growing in His knowledge and say that his life had never been better or had more purpose.

Paul literally flushed his vain religion down the toilet. He said that he never really knew God until he gained real knowledge through a real relationship with Christ Jesus. All the old religion was not real at all. It was just dead works. Nothing is sadder than being in a dead religion and knowing it. People know when they are a part of something that is truly without life. It would be wonderful indeed if all Christians felt as Paul did, but sadly many never count all loss for Christ. It is sad that many Christians will trade back their relationship with Christ for the old life. Paul spoke to Timothy of those who will *"wax wanton against Christ."* He said they would begin to cast off their faith and go back to the old life. Remember how many of the children of Israel wanted to go back to Egypt after God had brought them out? No, we must follow Paul and leave all behind to follow Jesus. That is what the first disciples did as well. *Luke 5:11 And when they had brought their ships to land, they forsook all, and followed him. Matthew 19:27 Then answered Peter and said unto him, Behold, we have forsaken all, and followed thee; what shall we have therefore?* The farther you go on with your Lord, the less attraction the old life holds.

Paul wanted to *"win Christ."* This is the very same Greek word as "gain." The more Paul knew of Christ, the more he desired to know Him better. He now begins to tell us how we can know Christ in the very best ways.

Many live shallow lives. Paul wanted his life to be found not just *with* Christ but *in* Christ. Paul is not doubting his salvation. He is speaking of a more perfect knowledge. You get out of life what you put into life. I grew up with a very strong desire to hunt. I never had the opportunity when I was growing up at home, but when I was a young man I finally got the opportunity to go. I started bow hunting deer. I knew nothing about it. I did not have any videos or books. I knew no one where I lived who could teach me anything. My father in law had given me an old Indian Shikar bow that he had bought at a garage sale. It was a dinosaur, but I loved it. I could shoot a dime at sixty yards, but I could almost outrun the arrow before it hit the target. That was using an old painted metal pin sight system. I put on an old military uniform and went out to some public ground an hour from our house. I did not walk in while it was still dark and wait for light. I walked in as the sun was coming up at first light. I did not know any better. I just started walking through the woods looking for what I thought might be a good spot. I found a spot where another hunter, who obviously knew no more than I did, had hung a wooden pallet in between two trees. It was only six feet off the ground. I pulled myself up and sat on a milk crate that had been left. Believe it or not, along came a young doe. It was just a yearling, but it could have been the biggest deer in the woods for all I knew. It looked at me, I looked at it, and then I shot it. I was successful to a degree, but I was never going to become a trophy hunter like I wanted without growing in my knowledge of deer hunting. Most hunters kill deer that are less than two years of age. Many will never kill a record book animal because they will never improve their skills and their knowledge. Trophy record book animals are at least three years of age. The biggest ones are usually over five years old. The young ones are always the first out and about. Their innocent curiosity has been the cause of their demise. My knowledge did grow through the years, but it came through diligence, research and some hard lessons. I have now killed several trophy animals. Again, you get out of your relationship with Jesus what you put into it. The ground is level at the foot of the cross, but there are those that do know Christ better than others because of what they have done with their relationship. This is not a "deeper" life. It is a "more" life. It is a life in Christ that goes beyond superficial Christianity and lives near the heart of God. If you would know Jesus better, it will take more prayer, more Bible reading, more time in church and more hard lessons.

Man's righteousness has never been enough for God. The righteousness of man always falls short of the glory of God. Paul had realized years ago that he would never be good enough for God on his own merit. *Isaiah 64:6 But we are all as an unclean thing, and all our righteousnesses are as filthy rags; and we all do fade as a leaf; and our iniquities, like the wind, have taken us away.* The righteousness of man condemns man because it cannot change our heart. The righteousness of God comes by faith and changes us from the inside out- 2 Corinthians 5:17. The righteousness of God only comes to man through the person and work of Jesus Christ. When we come to God in faith for salvation, God places the righteousness of Jesus upon us. It is called "imparted" or "imputed" righteousness. I have an uncle who is only four years older than me. When I was a boy I got all his hand-me-downs. He was the only child left at home and the child of my grandparents old age. He had better clothes than I had. I could not wait to get them. Whenever he got something new that I liked, I would think to myself, "I am going to get that shirt eventually," and I almost always did. God looks on my ragged old clothes of righteousness and says these will never do. He brings us the garment of Christ's righteousness and puts it on us so that we may be properly clothed in Him.

That garment of righteousness which was worn to shreds on Adam's back will never make a covering for mine. ~D.L. Moody

Paul's Passionate Pursuit- Philippians 3:10-11

Philippians 3:10-11 *That I may know him, and the power of his resurrection, and the fellowship of his sufferings, being made conformable unto his death; If by any means I might attain unto the resurrection of the dead.*

There was something that Paul had not yet attained. He had not attained the prize of his resurrection. He mentions it both first and last in these two verses. He was not yet perfect or fully sanctified and glorified. He was still in a mortal body with an old nature.

Paul wanted to know Jesus in some very specific ways. He sets them before us here. He is telling us that this is what it really means to know Jesus Christ in a real way. Again, there is an intellectual knowledge and there is also a knowledge of personal experience. To know Christ by personal experience would be a personal knowledge of a personal Savior. Paul would know his Savior intimately and not as some far off God in the heavens that really did not care about Paul. A living religion will produce a living relationship. God did not create man just to keep rules. God created man for fellowship. Keeping God's rules are important, and I firmly believe that rules are based on relationships. The Garden of Eden shows us the pattern, but far too many are just trying to keep the rules without really knowing God.

Even personal devotions often times becomes more of a duty than a delight.

Paul wanted to know the power of Jesus' resurrection. Only then would Paul be brought into a perfect and complete fellowship with Jesus Christ. Jesus had been resurrected from the dead. Paul longed for the day when Christ would resurrect him from the dead. *Romans 8:11 But if the Spirit of him that raised up Jesus from the dead dwell in you, he that raised up Christ from the dead shall also quicken your mortal bodies by his Spirit that dwelleth in you.* We often sing the song *Because* "He Lives." Because Christ lives, I live. Christ is resurrected. I shall be resurrected. Because Jesus lives, I can know Him personally and have purpose and power for living. A living Christ makes a sacred life for us even as we live on earth.

Paul also wanted to know the fellowship of Christ's sufferings. Now Paul had been suffering for Christ for many years. Paul learned that as he suffered for Christ, he was brought into a greater knowledge of Christ and a deeper fellowship. Remember Paul was imprisoned as he penned this. He was saying he wanted more suffering so that he would know Christ better. The suffering was a small price to pay for the knowledge of Christ he would gain. Paul did not self-inflict suffering upon himself, but he did embrace his divinely appointed sufferings for Christ. There are not many Christians who really desire to know Christ in this way. The truth is you will never really know Christ until you suffer. To suffer for Jesus is not a punishment. It is a privilege. You never share in the work of Christ unless you share in His sufferings. We have countless verses to teach us this. *1 Peter 2:21 For even hereunto were ye called: because Christ also suffered for us, leaving us an example, that ye should follow his steps. 2 Corinthians 4:10-11 Always bearing about in the body the dying of the Lord Jesus, that the life also of Jesus might be made manifest in our body. For we which live are alway delivered unto death for Jesus' sake, that the life also of Jesus might be made manifest in our mortal flesh. Galatians 6:17 From henceforth let no man trouble me: for I bear in my body the marks of the Lord Jesus. Colossians 1:24 Who now rejoice in my sufferings for you, and fill up that which is behind of the afflictions of Christ in my flesh for his body's sake, which is the church. 2 Timothy 2:12 If we suffer, we shall also reign with him: if we deny him, he also will deny us. 1 Peter 4:13 But rejoice, inasmuch as ye are partakers of Christ's sufferings; that, when his glory shall be revealed, ye may be glad also with exceeding joy.* Suffering brings us closer to Christ. It makes us know Him better. If you do not know the sufferings of Christ, you will not be prepared to serve Him in the way He has chosen for you. There are three things that make you more like Jesus than anything else-suffering, prayer, and forgiveness to those who have wronged you.

There is no fellowship so precious as that which one has with a close and intimate friend in his sufferings. ~Dr. Lehman Strauss

Paul said that he must know what it meant to be conformed to the death of Christ. Why does he speak of the resurrection first and then of the death of Jesus? Should not the resurrection appear last? These are not out of order. Paul did not get the cart ahead of the horse. He is not speaking historically. He is speaking experientially. He had partaken of Christ's resurrection first in his regeneration. Now he must live by dying daily to the old man putting on the new each day. *Ephesians 4:20-23 But ye have not so learned Christ; If so be that ye have heard him, and have been taught by him, as the truth is in Jesus: That ye put off concerning the former conversation the old man, which is corrupt according to the deceitful lusts; And be renewed in the spirit of your mind.*

The Greek word for conformed is *summorphoo*. It means to be "formed like" or "fashioned like." This is what Paul also told the church at Rome. *Romans 8:29 For whom he did foreknow, he also did predestinate to be conformed to the image of his Son, that he might be the firstborn among many brethren.* God wants each of us to be fashioned just like Jesus. The best way to be like Jesus is to die to self. Paul told the church at Corinth that he died daily. Dr. John R. Rice used to say that every day you have to nail self to the cross. He said when you get up the next morning you will find that old booger has slipped down, and you will have to nail him up there again. To know Christ is to die to self every day and walk in the resurrection power of Christ through His Holy Spirit. Jesus told us to deny ourselves daily and take up our daily cross. To live in the power of the resurrection is to become more and more dead to the ways of the world. It is to crucify the flesh with lusts and affections thereof- Galatians 5:22.

174

There are those who claim this verse teaches that you can attain the resurrection by any means. You can get to heaven anyway you want. Of course, you have to disregard the preceding and following verses to do this, which is bad Bible exposition. Verse eleven is the final part of one complete sentence structure that began in verse seven. You cannot build a religion out of one sentence, let alone one verse that is only one part of a sentence. You have to take the whole passage in context. Always remember that a text without a context is just a pretext. In Paul's day there were those who claimed the resurrection was already past. Most notably Hymenaeus and Philetus are recorded in Scripture to have led such company. Paul had not yet fully apprehended Christ. He uses the word "attain" here in verses eleven and twelve. The word attain also means "arrive." Paul is saying that if there is any way to arrive at the resurrection it is by the means of verse ten. In order to arrive in the manner just spoken of, Paul would have to run according to what he now speaks of in verses twelve through sixteen. He has to forget all he has done in the past and fix his eyes on Christ his prize and run until he arrives.

Paul's Precious Prize- Philippians 3:12-16

Philippians 3:12-16 *Not as though I had already attained, either were already perfect: but I follow after, if that I may apprehend that for which also I am apprehended of Christ Jesus. Brethren, I count not myself to have apprehended: but this one thing I do, forgetting those things which are behind, and reaching forth unto those things which* *are before, I press toward the mark for the prize of the high calling of God in Christ Jesus. Let us therefore, as many as be perfect, be thus minded: and if in any thing ye be otherwise minded, God shall reveal even this unto you. Nevertheless, whereto we have already attained, let us walk by the same rule, let us mind the same thing.*

There are those who claim that they have arrived at a point of sinless perfection here in this life on earth. If Paul had not reached that point, I sincerely doubt anyone else ever has. Paul discredits this in his letter to the church at Thessalonica. *1 Thessalonians 5:23 And the very God of peace sanctify you wholly; and I pray God your whole spirit and soul and body be preserved blameless unto the coming of our Lord Jesus Christ.* Paul would not have needed to pray for the church to be blameless if they already were blameless. Sanctification is the growth process of the Christian life until we become complete in Him. It is a continuous growth that will not be complete until we get to heaven. *2 Peter 3:18 But grow in grace, and in the knowledge of our Lord and Saviour Jesus Christ. To him be glory both now and for ever. Amen.*

Isaiah was the best Christian on the earth in his day and when he saw the throne of God all he could see was his exceeding sinfulness. He cried out that he was an unclean man dwelling in the midst of an unclean people.

Those who claim to be sinless now, to have already attained perfection of spirit, only advertise their guilty distance from God and put themselves into an attitude of direct conflict with the scriptures. Making such a claim in this life shows that the one making it is in a dim light. ~Dr. B. H. Carroll

Paul had not yet attained or "arrived" at his goal yet. He was not yet perfect in the eternal sense of a glorified body and a fully sanctified spirit. Paul had not reached a resurrection type glorified body while here on the earth. His final destination or prize would be eternally dwelling with Jesus Christ fully sanctified and glorified. Paul desired to be perfect- *teleioo.* This word for perfect means "completed" or "finished" or "brought to a full end." Paul's life in Christ would not be complete until he was both fully sanctified and glorified. He had not apprehended these things though Christ had apprehended (gotten hold of) him. He had not yet attained, but that is the prize that he is pressing towards. As long as he was on the earth, he simply pressed towards that goal. He could follow after Christ. He could pursue the prize Christ had waiting for him until one day he would finally apprehend that prize and claim it as his own.

In verse thirteen, Paul had one thing on his mind and one thing alone. He wanted to finish the life God had given him in the manner God would have him to do so. Many folks have what we would call a specialty. They can do many things that many can do, but they have a specialty skill that is not common to others. It is the one thing they are an expert in. We are not short of experts in our churches today. Some are experts at memorizing sports statistics. Others are experts at video games. Others are experts in their ability to fix computers. We have experts in economics, statistics, politics and all the other "tics." We have too many that are expert at something that amounts to nothing in the eyes of God. Christians ought to be experts at being Christians.

Paul needed to forget the old life for two reasons. First, he needed to forget past achievements. Past achievements keep you from future success. Many who live in former glories waste the rest of their life never doing anything for God when oftentimes their greatest work is still before them. God does not waste a day of human life. God does not look at us and say, "You did a good job today. Take the rest of your life off." Hebrews 4:11 tells us that we labor to enter into rest. As long as we are here, we have some future service for the Lord. In order to reach forth we need to forget those things that are behind and not live in the glories of days gone by. This very thing is what killed the church of Sardis- Revelation 3:1.

Second, Paul needed to forget the sins of his past. Someone once said, "The load of tomorrow added to that of yesterday, and carried today, makes the strongest falter." He had persecuted and wasted the church of God. He had imprisoned believers and consented to the murder of Stephen and probably others. Paul mentions these blights on his record in several of his letters. Many people have a past that wants to haunt them. It is impossible for a finite mind to not remember the past, but we may bring every thought into captivity to the obedience of Christ- 2 Corinthians 10:5. Paul needed to forget the old way of self-righteousness and walk in newness of life in Christ. The past was done and could not be changed. He must reach forth to the prize Christ had set before him. He could never attain his prize if he clung to his past. One of the great tricks of the Devil is to discourage Christians into thinking they can never be of any value or service to God because of their past. It has been often said that when the devil reminds us of our past failures, we should remind him of his future doom. God removes our sin so that we may serve Him without the guilt of the past. That is justification- being made "just as if I had never sinned." Christ has redeemed us, purchased us, and with that purchase He has justified us (Romans 3:24)- removed the guilt of our sin. God does not hold our past sins against us. To do so would not be true forgiveness. The blood of Jesus cleanses us from sin (1 John 1:7-12)- washes it away as if it was never there. I love what Dr. Rice used to say.

No matter what a man's past, his future is spotless. When the devil reminds you of your past, remind him of his future. ~Dr. John R. Rice

Paul said he was *"reaching forth"* which carries the idea of one that has his eyes fixed on the goal line. No good Christian can ever be satisfied in his present spiritual state. We must continue to reach forth. Remember Lot's wife? She looked back to Sodom and was turned into a pillar of salt. She never finished her race because her eyes were not fixed on the deliverance God set before her. Jesus told the disciples to leave the old life and never look back. *Luke 9:62 And Jesus said unto him, No man, having put his hand to the plough, and looking back, is fit for the kingdom of God.* We must keep our eye on the prize and run flat out for the finish line.

In verse fourteen Paul acknowledges the fact that he has a divine calling. We have record of it in Acts 9, and Paul referred to it throughout his life- Acts 22:6-10; 26:12-19. There are many calls that come to men in this mortal life. The world will call to us in many ways. The world calls us to live for the moment. The world calls us to live for self. The world calls to us and tells us that we may put God off and answer His call later in life. The world calls us with its cares and concerns. The world calls to us to take pleasure in all she has to offer.

Then there is the call of God. There is no higher calling than the divine calling of the Creator to the creature and from the Redeemer to His redeemed. God calls to every man to be saved- Acts 17:30, 1 Peter 3:9. Then God calls every man to service- Ephesians 2:10. God calls to us to come from the world and be separate- 2 Corinthians 6:17-18. God calls us to holiness- 1 Peter 1:15-16. God calls us to love- John 13:35; 1 John 3:23. God calls every man to be *in* Christ Jesus. Yes, there are earthly calls, and there are heavenly calls.

Heaven calls us to a prize that wins Christ. God calls us to the starting line once we are saved. The race is set before us and we must run it with patience. Our goal is before us- to win Jesus Christ. He has apprehended (saved) us. We must fixate our eyes upon Him and run until we reach Him. That prize will become a reality to us at the resurrection for all who are awake or sleep in Him. Our prize is the completed sanctification of our spirit and the glorification of a new body. It is to be eternally in the presence of our Lord and Savior Jesus Christ. Our prize is getting to where Christ is now- in heaven seated at the right hand of the Father. No one is judged by what they have done after they have died. We will be judged by the deeds we have done up to the time of our death. In order to hear "well done" we must have done well.

There is no tragedy so great as a Christian at the end of life's journey with the bitter knowledge that he failed to achieve that for which his Lord saved him. ~Dr. Lehman Strauss

I want to finish well. I once read a story that was told by Dr. E. Schuyler English that I believe illustrates what Paul was expressing in verses thirteen and fourteen. "Looking through the porthole of our cabin early in the morning, as the *Kungsholm* approached Padan Bay, Bali, we were able to see majestic Genung Agung, one of the highest mountains in Indonesia, its peak rising 10,000 feet into the blue, cloudless sky. We wondered how many times its summit had been reached and whether anyone had lost his life in the attempt. This brought to mind something a friend in England told us several years ago. In a small churchyard at the foot of one of the great mountains of Switzerland, the body of a young Englishman, who was killed while making an ascent, is buried. On the tombstone, under his name and the dates of his birth and death, the following inscription is carved: "HE DIED CLIMBING."

Paul said that he had not attained perfection in verse twelve, but now speaks of it as one having obtained. This is not a contradiction. In verse twelve Paul speaks of eternal perfection. Verse fifteen speaks of earthly perfection. In verse twelve Paul spoke of final perfection in an eternal glorified state. In verse fifteen he is speaking of a mature or developmental perfection here on the earth. He wanted to be an adult Christian not a babe in Christ. This is not a sinless perfection but a perfection that makes us complete to perform the task. Paul had been saved for nearly thirty years. He had grown in grace and knowledge. He was fully equipped to function in the ministry God had given him. He was qualified to perform the task God had given him. You would not want a first year med student taking out your gall bladder, but a doctor who has completed (perfected) his training and has his degree is qualified. Paul was not a novice. He was mature in Christ. Paul's letter would be read by perfect (mature) Christians and imperfect (immature) Christians. This statement is for those who are mature in Christ. As a little child, someone is doing everything for you. As an adult, you must discipline yourself to do what you are supposed to do. No one is going to do for you what you can now do for yourself.

A "thus minded" Christian will be a single minded Christian. They are those who focus on the task at hand. We need to focus on "one thing" and forget about all the "other things." We need to have the mindset to press toward the mark. There always seem to be "other things" in life. These are the "what if's" and "what about" or the "how do I" and "should I or should I not" questions of life. Some never run the race because they are consumed with the "what if's" and "what might be's" of life. They want a contingency plan for everything that may or may not lie before them. They are like the man who hid his talent in the earth and did nothing with the opportunity his Lord had given him for fear that he would do the wrong thing. God will reveal or answer all of life's questions regarding "other things" as you run with your eyes fixated on Christ. He will give you knowledge to make right decision in the moment you need to make a decision and not before. God reveals all things to us through His Spirit. *John 16:13 Howbeit when he, the Spirit of truth, is come, he will guide you into all truth: for he shall not speak of himself; but whatsoever he shall hear, [that] shall he speak: and he will shew you things to come. 1 Corinthians 2:9-10 But as it is written, Eye hath not seen, nor ear heard, neither have entered into the heart of man, the things which God hath prepared for them that love him. But God hath revealed them unto us by his Spirit: for the Spirit searcheth all things, yea, the deep things of God.* Child of God, let God do the leading and the teaching in your life. *Psalms 32:9 Be ye not as the horse, or as the mule, which have no understanding: whose mouth must be held in with bit and bridle, lest they come near unto thee.* Even God warns us not to be stubborn as a mule or a horse that has to have the bit in its mouth to be led. Keep a teachable spirit. Keep a tender spirit to the voice of Holy Spirit in you.

In verse sixteen Paul tells us that we have come this far or arrived safely this far by keeping our eyes fixed on Christ. We have come safely because we have had a "one track" mind and goal. Let this continue to be the rule of life. Do not begin to change how you run your course as you near the finish line. Keep running by the same rule. Keep minding (walking obediently) to the same thing that has got you this far. Jesus was worth beginning this race. He is worth finishing this race. Keep on keeping on.

Paul's Plea for Perfection- Philippians 3:17-21

Philippians 3:17-21 *Brethren, be followers together of me, and mark them which walk so as ye have us for an ensample. (For many walk, of whom I have told you often, and now tell you even weeping, that they are the enemies of the cross of Christ: Whose end is destruction, whose God is their belly, and whose glory is in their shame, who mind earthly things.) For our conversation is in heaven; from whence also we look for the Saviour, the Lord Jesus Christ: Who shall change our vile body, that it may be fashioned like unto his glorious body, according to the working whereby he is able even to subdue all things unto himself.*

These verses set two examples before us. One is to be followed. One is to be shunned. Paul sets himself as an example to be followed. He then tells the church to shun those who serve themselves under the pretense of serving God. We have so little time to serve and suffer with our Lord. One old preacher said that "time is the training school for the ages to come." We must remember that the time God has allotted us is brief and precious. It should be given wholly unto Him.

Remember the difference between example and ensample? An example is what pattern we follow. An ensample is which person we follow. Paul said that he and his fellow helpers were the right ones to follow after. Every parent wants their child to follow good ensamples. Paul made sure to be the right ensample so that he knew the people of Philippi would have someone to follow after. The word ensample also means "an impression" or "a mark made by a blow." Jesus made an impression on my life that changed me forever. Jesus struck a blow that conquered sin and death for every man on Calvary. My life will be used to make an impression on someone else. Every parent makes an impact (strike a blow) that will leave an impression on their children for the rest of their lives. The same can be said for Sunday School teachers, children's church workers, Master Clubs teachers, bus workers and all other servants and soul winners of Jesus Christ. The Bible teaches us that no man lives to himself and no man dies to himself. Your life may be the only Bible some will ever read. Be careful not to leave a bad or a false impression. Far too many have struck a bad blow. Be sure to make a good impression on others for Jesus Christ.

Paul asked us to be followers of him. He also says "them" and "us," which would appear to include Paul's current companions- Luke, Timothy, Epaphroditus, Silas and probably some others as well. Paul's plea was not a plea of pride. Paul lived what he preached. Paul was following Jesus. He wanted the Philippians to follow Jesus also. The word follow is the Greek word *summimetes.* It means "fellow-imitators." Paul was imitating Christ or following Christ's example. He desired for the church at Philippi to follow-imitate-Christ with him. They would be fellow-imitators of Jesus Christ together. They were not following behind Paul. They were following Christ with Paul.

Paul could not please everyone. Every pastor learns this lesson sooner or later. *Galatians 1:10 For do I now persuade men, or God? or do I seek to please men? for if I yet pleased men, I should not be the servant of Christ.* Why would anyone want to follow Paul? His life was one of constant peril, persecution, poverty and prison. Paul had contemptible speech. His appearance left nothing to be desired. His work was criticized and his apostleship denied. He was accused of being a deceiver. No true servant of Christ will walk without enemies or false accusation. In spite of all these false accusations and a life that no one in this world would desire, he knew he could please Christ. Paul preached Christ and lived Christ. That is the faith we follow. Paul was not perfect, but he was a good ensample to follow.

I have ever to confess, with sorrow, that I am far from being what I ought to be, and far from what I wish to be, but also-blessed by God's Name!- to testify that I am far, very far, from what I once was. ~John Newton

And though centuries have rolled by since wicked men sought to dishonor him, and the executioner's axe severed his hoary head from his body by Caesar's order, thus finishing his testimony in laying down his life for his Master's sake, he still remains the pre-eminent example of what the Christian should be, sustained by grace divine while passing through this valley of death's shadow. Let us examine our own ways and see how they measure up to his- not excusing ourselves for failure on the score that times and conditions have changed from those that surrounded him. The same One who wrought effectually in him so long ago, will work in us today if there be but a willing mind and a sanctified determination to take his path of unworldliness and devotion to Christ. ~Dr. Henry Ironside

It literally brought Paul to tears that the cross has so many enemies. Jesus wept over the city of Jerusalem. *Matthew 23:37 O Jerusalem, Jerusalem, thou that killest the prophets, and stonest them which are sent unto thee, how often would I have gathered thy children together, even as a hen gathereth her chickens under her wings, and ye would not!* Jesus knew that the religious crowd was soon to crucify Him when all He desired was to draw His own close to Him. The cross has never been without enemies. You can always tell the enemy of the cross. Their god is not the God of heaven. Their god is their own belly. One man said this, "The golden calf has been cast into a different form today. One look at our gorging, our garments, and our gadgets and a voice says: These be thy gods." They will always fill their belly to the starvation of others. They are selfish and not sacrificial. They do not desire to bring any glory to God. They want all glory for themselves. They give themselves wholly to self-gratification and instant gratification. B.H. Carroll once said that he did not know any worse enemy of the cross than the Antinomians. These are they who claim Christian liberty gives them the right to live as they please. They sin that grace may abound. These desire the death benefits of Christ that they might continue to live in the shame of sin. They want salvation without repentance. They turn liberty into licentiousness (every evil lust). They claim that Christians may ascend to all the spiritual heights of salvation, and yet it is lawful to descend back into the depths of sin as well. They claim that since grace abounds greater than anyone's sins, people could sin as they like and not worry. It makes no difference to an all-forgiving God. *Romans 6:1-2 What shall we say then? Shall we continue in sin, that grace may abound? God forbid. How shall we, that are dead to sin, live any longer therein? Romans 6:11 Likewise reckon ye also yourselves to be dead indeed unto sin, but alive unto God through Jesus Christ our Lord. Galatians 5:1 Stand fast therefore in the liberty wherewith Christ hath made us free, and be not entangled again with the yoke of bondage. Galatians 5:13 For, brethren, ye have been called unto liberty; only [use] not liberty for an occasion to the flesh, but by love serve one another. 1Peter 2:16 As free, and not using [your] liberty for a cloke of maliciousness, but as the servants of God. 2Peter 2:19 While they promise them liberty, they themselves are the servants of corruption: for of whom a man is overcome, of the same is he brought in bondage.* Grace is not a license to sin. It is a higher calling to a holy life. True liberty always has limitations.

To me the most horrible thing in the world is for a man to profess belief in the high doctrines of grace and then live an evil life. ~B.H. Carroll

Professing Christians who use Christianity as an excuse for lawlessness are a threat to the testimony of the church. ~Dr. Lehman Strauss

These who pervert the Gospel (Galatians 1:7) lead others to follow them to destruction. Mahatma Gandhi was born in 1869. He became the great leader of India during her time of British rule and eventually led India to her independence. His influence for freedom and civil rights was world-wide. He once told of how he had spent years studying every major religion in the world at that time. After he examined all the great religions of the world, he made this statement: "I would be a Christian if it were not for Christians." The Christians whose example caused Ghandi to make this statement are just as guilty of his death as the man that assassinated him in 1948. The end of all who live in this way is destruction. Jesus told of a man who pulled down his barns to build greater. *Luke 12:19-20 And I will say to my soul, Soul, thou hast much goods laid up for many years; take thine ease, eat, drink, and be merry. But God said unto him, Thou fool, this*

189

night thy soul shall be required of thee: then whose shall those things be, which thou hast provided? It is all summed up in these four words *"Who mind earthly things."* The Bible tells us that man is of the earth. The nature of the earthly is to root around the earth much like a pig does. When a man gets saved, his whole life and nature is changed. He now has a heavenly nature. With that nature comes a new conversation. That is a new life and citizenship. A true child of God will have no more love for earthly things than their Savior did. Our Savior's life was not bound by the things of earth. Christ was no materialist. Paul has already told us that he held no earthly things dear to himself. The church needs more like Mary of Bethany who chose the better part of sitting at the feet of Jesus.

Cicero complained of Homer that he taught the gods to live like men. Grace teaches men to live like God. ~D.L. Moody

Paul reminds us in verse twenty of our conversation. Remember the word conversation is the Greek word *politeuma.* This is where we get our English words citizen, policeman and politics. Remember that Philippi was a Roman colony. It was filled with retired Roman soldiers who earned their citizenship by service to Rome. These men were given all the rights and privileges of a free-born citizen of Rome. Even though they lived in Philippi, they could say that their citizenship was in Rome. They dressed like Romans, spoke Latin like Romans, used Roman titles and cultural distinctions. Their justice was Roman as were their morals and lack of morality. They were never to forget what was expected of them as citizens of Rome. Let us apply the same principle to Christianity. Paul was saying that just as these Roman colonists never forget they belong to Rome, we must never forget that we belong to Christ in heaven. Our conversation- *politeuma*- and our spiritual citizenship is in heaven. Christians are to live on earth as Christ lives in heaven. We are not to wait until we get to heaven to lead a heavenly life. We are to lead a heavenly life now. We are expected to live by heavenly principles now. Remember that we cannot expect the citizens of this world to understand our heavenly conversation. The life of a Christian looks just as odd to this world as the life of the eastern hemisphere appears odd to a man from the western hemisphere. Everything appears strange that is not normal to his life.

We look to our Savior, the Lord Jesus Christ. Paul used all four New Testament titles of Jesus. He reminded us of the humanity of Christ. He reminds us of the Lordship of Christ Who has the right to rule and reign over His people. He reminds us that our salvation is from Christ. He reminds us that this Jesus is the Christ of God. Jesus is the Father's appointed choice to be Savior and Lord over all mankind. Far too many claim a Savior but deny their Lord.

Our body is vile. His is glorious. The word *vile* means "of low estate." These bodies are bodies of humility. The body of Christ is a body of glory that has been exalted. All saints must live with and suffer with the effects of our mortality, but there is coming a day when Jesus will ransom us from the power of sin, sickness, pain, death and the grave. The word *fashioned* is a word that is based on the word regeneration. One day Christ will take these low life bodies of ours and regenerate them to be made just like unto His. When Christ makes our body as His, we will be in perfect subjection to Him. It is the nature of these vile earthly bodies to rebel against their Creator. These vile bodies are of low estate or corruption. They are very frail and limited. Our heavenly body will be an eternal body without any weakness, corruption or imperfection.

The body is a clanking chain, that holds us down when we would fain rise, so that one understands something of what chained eagles feel, when they fret against the iron bars of their cage, and pine to soar on outspread pinions to the sun. ~F.B. Meyer

Chapter 4
Rejoicing In Christ's Provision

In chapter 4 Paul pleads with the church not to let personal preferences and self-interests hinder the work of the church. Paul will remind the church that the same power that saved the saints is available to solve all problems amongst the saints. Nothing is beyond the power of God. *Therefore*, yokes the Christ-like example of chapter three with the practicality of daily living in chapter four. Paul will also teach us that joy is the *source* of power, prayer is the *secret* of power and meditation on Christ is the *sanctuary* of power. Paul gives us three secrets to his joy in this chapter.

1. Paul rejoiced in Christ's coming.
2. Paul rejoiced in Christ through unceasing prayer.
3. Paul rejoiced in Christ by being thankful.

Philippi's Problem- Philippians 4:1-3

Philippians 4:1-3 *Therefore, my brethren dearly beloved and longed for, my joy and crown, so stand fast in the Lord, my dearly beloved. I* *beseech Euodias, and beseech Syntyche, that they be of the same mind in the Lord. And I intreat thee also, true yokefellow, help those women which laboured with me in the gospel, with Clement also, and with other my fellowlabourers, whose names are in the book of life.*

Paul uses the phrase *in the Lord* eight times in this short epistle. He uses it three times in the first four verses of chapter four:

1. Stand fast in the Lord.
2. Be of the same mind in the Lord.
3. Rejoice in the Lord.

The church at Philippi was dear to Paul's heart. He longed to be with them. The world of Christianity is very small, but it reaches out to the entire world. Missionaries, pastors and sojourning speakers often come through the doors of our church. They are here for a little while and then they go on their way. Many loved ones go to heaven ahead of us. We never know when we are seeing someone for the last time. We long to see them again. We shall see them soon. Very soon we will be eternally dwelling together in the presence of Jesus never again to be separated from those we love. Hold those you count dear to your heart close by continuing in prayer for them. Praying for those you hold dear to your heart and those you long to see, keeps your prayers from becoming a vain repetition.

This verse is a parallel passage to Paul's message to the Thessalonians. *1 Thessalonians 2:19-20 For what is our hope, or joy, or crown of rejoicing? Are not even ye in the presence of our Lord Jesus Christ at his coming? For ye are our glory and joy.* One day Paul will stand before God and receive the rewards of this life. Paul will see converts from the churches we read about in the Bible from all over Europe and Asia standing as saints of God. His reward will be those he has brought with him.

There are two words for crown in the New Testament. There is the word *diadema* which means the "royal crown." This is the crown of kingship. Then there is the word *stephanos*. The latter word is used by Paul in this verse. It has two background descriptions. First, it was the victor's crown awarded to athletes at the Greek games. It was made of wild olive leaves, interwoven with parsley and bay leaves. History states that in Ancient Greece, beginning in 776 BC, wreaths of laurel leaves crowned the victors of the athletic competitions and of the ancient Olympic games. Wreaths of bay laurels were also awarded at the Ancient Greek Pythian Games, which were held at Delphi in honor of Apollo (every four years from the 6th century BC). According to Greek Mythology, Apollo, the Olympian god and son of Zeus, was in love with a nymph named Daphne. The story tells us that Daphne fled from Apollo. After asking the river god for help, she was turned into a Bay Laurel tree just as Apollo approached her. Apollo embraced the tree, cut off a branch to wear as a wreath and declared the plant sacred. Thus, this myth spurred the presentation of the laurel wreaths, in honor of Apollo, to the victors of these games. (This also makes

Apollo the first tree hugger.) The phrase "resting on your laurels" is a reference to resting on your past accomplishments.

The second background of this crown is that it was placed upon the head of a guest at a banquet at some time of great joy. There is an old song that says the only thing that is better than going to heaven is taking someone with you. Paul knew that great joy. Paul was saying that the Philippians were the crown of his earthly toil. Paul would one day receive his victor's crown. Philippi would be a portion of his eternal reward and joy. *Psalms 126:6 He that goeth forth and weepeth, bearing precious seed, shall doubtless come again with rejoicing, bringing his sheaves with him.*

Paul knew there would be a day that they would be reunited in the presence of the Lord. He pleads for them to stand fast in the Lord until that time. The word *stand fast* is a military command. It is the command for soldiers to stand and hold the line as the enemy approaches. They are to wait for the command to attack as the enemy comes bearing down upon them. An overwhelming enemy force is advancing upon us- stand fast! Hold your ground. We may stand fast in the Lord because He is our power. *Ephesians 6:10 Finally, my brethren, be strong in the Lord, and in the power of his might.* The Bible tells us to meddle not with them that are given to change. So many have changed the principles by which they have lived and forsaken the old time religion for modernism. We are to stand faithful and true to the Lord by standing fast in the Lord. D.L. Moody used to tell of an old man who had gone to California to see his sons who had become rich.

196

On being asked to go to the theater, he said he had traveled far, but not far enough to forget his principles.

- ✝ Stand fast in the *faith* that is in Christ- 1 Corinthians 16:13.
- ✝ Stand fast in the *fellowship* that is in Christ- Philippians 1:27.
- ✝ Stand fast in the *freedom* that is in Christ- Galatians 5:1.
- ✝ Stand fast in the *foundations* that are in Christ- 2 Thessalonians 2:15.

In verses two and three we finally come to these two women we have already referenced several times. Euodias and Syntyche were two women in the church who had a disagreement. Evidently, the disagreement was a big enough problem that Paul felt the need to rebuke them in this epistle. Euodias means *fragrance.* Syntyche means *fortunate.* These were two good women who had labored much with Paul in the Gospel, but they had a disagreement. They allowed their differences to become a source of division and contention in the church. *James 4:1 From whence come wars and fightings among you? come they not hence, even of your lusts that war in your members?* It is a sober reminder to us that two ladies with sweet names and many good works for the Gospel, developed a testimony that is eternally blemished by bickering. It is interesting that the strife of these two women had to be addressed by Paul because women were very much a part of the background of Greek culture and not the forefront. The Greeks taught that a respectable woman should "see little, hear little

197

and ask as little as possible." A respectable woman never went out into the street alone. She was always accompanied by someone. She had her own room in the house. She never joined the male members of the family- even for meals. She had no part in public life. It must have been a great conflict to disrupt a church in a place where the culture kept the ladies so silent. We would never have known these two women were it not for their bickering. A bickering church is no church at all.

These two women also teach us that no matter how silent one's place in the church may be, we still have a great impact. If you read carefully through the book of Acts, you will find that the ladies are mentioned in every church. Thessalonica was a city where women were given a part in society and in labor. Paul won many of the "chief women" to Christ in that city and also Berea- Acts 17:4, 12. It is impossible for a church to fully function without the service of good Christian women. Consider the many works of the ladies of the church. They guide the house and raise the next generation of the church. A woman's greatest soul winning opportunity is found in her own home. Many second and third generation believers have come to Christ because of the prayers and godly influence of mothers and grandmothers, just as Timothy did. They pray silently in the church, but their prayers are heard just as clearly as a man's by the Father in heaven. They care for the nursery and teach many of the Sunday school and other classes for the children. They teach in Primary, Junior and Children's churches. They serve in choir and special music and prepare countless meals to feed guest preachers, the sick and those who mourn at funerals. These are just a small part of the great works of ladies in the church.

We do not know what it was that divided these two co-laborers. It really does not matter. It was not a point of major doctrinal error, or Paul would have set the record straight. There have been endless divisions in the church that can only be blamed on pigheaded pride. You have two good people with two different points of view. There is nothing wrong with either one except for the fact that someone is going to have to yield. People do not have to see eye to eye on every point in order to labor together for God. There is room for originality of thought. There is room for differences of administrations and diversities of operations- 1 Corinthians 12:5-6. We do not have to look at everything from the same standpoint. We each have varying educational and philosophical backgrounds. God can use all of our differences to accomplish one great task in fulfilling the Great Commission. It has been said that no two men have ever seen the same rainbow. We do, however, need to get along in order to get farther along in the work of Christ. If we take the mind of Christ- the lowly mind of humility- we will each prefer one another beyond ourselves. *Romans 12:10 [Be] kindly affectioned one to another with brotherly love; in honour preferring one another. 1Timothy 5:21 I charge [thee] before God, and the Lord Jesus Christ, and the elect angels, that thou observe these things without preferring one before another, doing nothing by partiality.* If every person in the church will seek to be like the Lord, we may have differences of judgment and preferences yet still possess peace and unity. Each member of the body of Christ may be different yet we are all still one in Him.

Remember that the church at Philippi started at a women's prayer meeting by the river- Acts 16:25-34. Lydia, a seller of purple, was the first convert. Euodias and Syntyche were possibly a part of that first meeting. Paul also mentions Clement (*merciful*) in verse three, who was most likely the pastor. Then he simply acknowledges other fellowlabourers, whose names are in the book of life. These were the first converts and workers of the church.

These two women also teach us that no matter how silent one's place in the church may be, we still have a great impact. If you read carefully through the book of Acts, you will find that the ladies are mentioned in every church. Thessalonica was a city where women were given a part in society and in labor. Paul won many of the "chief women" to Christ in that city and also Berea- Acts 17:4, 12. It is impossible for a church to fully function without the service of good Christian women. Consider the many works of the ladies of the church- they guide the house and raise the next generation of the church. A woman's greatest soul winning opportunity is found in her own home. Many second and third generation believers have come to Christ because of the prayers and godly influence of mothers and grandmothers. They pray silently in the church but their prayers are heard just as clearly as a man's by the Father in heaven. They care for the nursery and many of the Sunday school and Master's Club classes for the children. They teach in Primary, Junior and Children's churches. They serve in choir and special music and prepare countless meals to feed guests preachers, the sick and those who mourn at funerals. These are just a small part of the great works of ladies in the church.

We do not know what it was that divided these two co-laborers. It really does not matter. It was obviously something so insignificant that it was not worth mentioning. It was not a point of major doctrinal error or Paul would have set the record straight. There have been endless divisions in the church that can only be blamed on pigheaded pride. You have two good people with two different points of view. There is nothing wrong with either one except for the fact that someone is going to have to yield. People do not have to see eye to eye on every point in order to labor together for God. There is room for originality of thought. There is room for differences of administrations and diversities of operations- 1 Corinthians 12:5-6. We do not have to look at everything from the same standpoint. We each have different educational and philosophical backgrounds. God can use all of our differences to accomplish one great task in fulfilling the Great Commission. It has been said that not two men ever saw the same rainbow.

Philippi's Peace- Philippians 4:4-9

Philippians 4:4-9 *Rejoice in the Lord alway: and again I say, Rejoice. Let your moderation be known unto all men. The Lord is at hand. Be careful for nothing; but in every thing by prayer and supplication with* *thanksgiving let your requests be made known unto God. And the peace of God, which passeth all understanding, shall keep your hearts and minds through Christ Jesus. Finally, brethren, whatsoever things are true, whatsoever things are honest, whatsoever things are just, whatsoever things are pure, whatsoever things are lovely, whatsoever things are of good report; if there be any virtue, and if there be any praise, think on these things. Those things, which ye have both learned, and received, and heard, and seen in me, do: and the God of peace shall be with you.*

Paul gives a simple but powerful command in verse four. Spirits were probably at an all-time low in the church. Strife grieves the Spirit of God- Ephesians 4:30. If the Holy Spirit is grieved within the church, the people will lose their joy. It is a simple truth that comes by observing human nature that one can be miserable in wealth, power and fame, while another is overflowing with real joy in spite of living in the depths of poverty. Captain Robert Scot of the Antarctic once wrote in a personal letter, "We are pegging out in every comfortless spot...We are in a desperate state-feet frozen, etc., no fuel, and a long way from food, but it would do your heart good to be in our tent, to hear our songs and our cheery conversation." Joy is not determined by the possession of earthly things. It is determined by Christ possessing you. *Luke 12:15 And he said unto them, Take heed, and beware of covetousness: for a man's life consisteth not in the abundance of the things which he possesseth.*

Rejoice always. What can be more than always? The word rejoice means to have repeated joy over and over again. *John 15:11 These things have I spoken unto you, that my joy might remain in you, and that your joy might be full.* Christians may rejoice always because Christ is always with us. We never need to lose our joy because we can never lose Christ. In good times and bad, through joy and sorrow, in gain and loss, rejoice always. Rejoice in the Lord and not in temporal pleasures, things or positions. Rejoice not in earthly things. Rejoice in the Lord. The Bible teaches us that we may rejoice in spite of varying adversity. Habakkuk says that we can rejoice in times of famine. *Habakkuk 3:17-18 Although the fig tree shall not blossom, neither shall fruit be in the vines; the labour of the olive shall fail, and the fields shall yield no meat; the flock shall be cut off from the fold, and there shall be no herd in the stalls: Yet I will rejoice in the LORD, I will joy in the God of my salvation.* Isaiah says that we may rejoice in times of poverty. *Isaiah 29:19 The meek also shall increase their joy in the LORD, and the poor among men shall rejoice in the Holy One of Israel.* Isaiah also tells us we may rejoice in times of judgment. *Isaiah 41:15-16 Behold, I will make thee a new sharp threshing instrument having teeth: thou shalt thresh the mountains, and beat them small, and shalt make the hills as chaff. Thou shalt fan them, and the wind shall carry them away, and the whirlwind shall scatter them: and thou shalt rejoice in the LORD, and shalt glory in the Holy One of Israel.* If you can rejoice in famine, poverty and judgment, you can rejoice always.

Joy will drive out the disunity. Joy is a slice of the fruit of the Spirit. Joy is a peacemaker. Joy is a burden lifter. A successful sales person will sell you something you neither want nor need simply by having a joyful spirit. They smile and tell you how wonderful their product is. Comedians make their millions by simply bringing laughter to people. People do want real joy. They are desperately trying to find it. The world has what it calls "happy hour." They hope that drinking will cause them to forget their problems for a few hours. I wonder how many folks have walked out of churches and into bars because they found the church to be cold, dry and lifeless. The world needs to see joy in Christians and the Church.

The presence of Jesus gives us a reason to rejoice. I have met Christians all over the world who will never own anything materially that anyone from our nation would desire to have, yet they are far happier than many Americans who claim Christ. When Jesus is all you have, joy is all you will know. Our material possessions and our covetousness are the greatest joy killers we will ever know. The presence of Jesus is brought near to us by the Holy Spirit within us. Charles Haddon Spurgeon said that he did not recollect spending a quarter of an hour without the distinct thought of the presence of Christ in his life. Spurgeon, a man who struggled all his life with serious bouts of depression, wrote these words about this verse:

† Joy is commanded because joy makes us like God.

† Joy is commanded because it is for our profit.

† Joy is commanded because it is good for others.

† Paul rejoiced to show his love to the church.

† Paul rejoiced to suggest the difficulty of continual joy. He twice commands because we are slow to obey.

† Paul rejoiced to assert the possibility of it.

† Paul rejoiced to impress the importance of the duty.

Written by a man in prison, who for thirty years had been mobbed, beaten, stoned, and cuffed about, enough to make the angels gasp. Yet he is overflowing with JOY. ~Henry Halley

The preceding verses posed a problem. Now, Paul sought to bring peace. God allows peace to follow our problems. In verse five Paul says to let us not be of that number who use the word moderation as a license to sin.   There is no Christ-like moderation nor pattern in gluttony, drunkenness, tobacco, drugs, gambling, etc. Moderation is not a balancing act for sin. It governs righteousness. Moderation is the balance that holds the scales of the Christian life. Moderation is a most neglected quality of the Christian life. It is the balance of the Christian life. It is our temperance.   To fall short in our Christianity is to compromise. To exceed in it is to become a cult. We do not need compromisers or cults either one. Some are all compassion without conviction. Others are all conviction without compassion. We need our convictions tempered with our compassion.   We need the moderation of Christianity. There are those who have mercy without justice and justice without mercy. Moderation is the balance beam that holds justice and mercy where they both belong. Moderation balances convictions and compassion.

Paul told these two woman that the Lord was watching so they better behave themselves and get along. You see to the Greek moderation was defined as "justice" or "something better than justice." There is the letter of the law and the spirit of the law. Both are important but the spirit of the law is most important to God. God is always first and foremost concerned about the attitude of the heart rather than the actions of humanity. You see justice must always have a provision for mercy. *Romans 2:28-29 For he is not a Jew, which is one outwardly; neither is that circumcision, which is outward in the flesh: But he is a Jew, which is one inwardly; and circumcision is that of the heart, in the spirit, and not in the letter; whose praise is not of men, but of God.* Opinion has no consideration for the needs and the feelings of others. Paul was not asking Euodias and Syntyche to sacrifice right for wrong. He was asking them to yield their preferences to maintain peace in the church.

Here is a simple illustration. Let us say two college students both take an exam. The papers are graded by the same standard. One student gets an eighty percent and another student gets a fifty percent. One passes, and one fails. That is the letter of the law. If we go beyond the examination and examine the two students we will find two different circumstances. The student who received an eighty percent worked in ideal conditions with a quiet place to study and adequate resources before him. That student has a calm and peaceful home with no external problems. The student who received a fifty percent struggles financially to pay the bill and is constantly carrying that burden. He does not have as much time to study because he has to work to support himself. It is discovered that this student's mother has cancer and the father has lost his job. In justice this student deserves the fifty percent but in moderation- something better than justice- this student probably studied harder than the student that received the eighty percent. The teacher might give the student with the failing grade a passing grade. The teacher has gone beyond the letter of the law and honored the spirit of justice by mercy.

We can see this Biblically as well. In John 8 a woman was taken in the act of adultery and brought to Jesus; however, she was taken hostage by a group of hypocrites whose hearts were far more sinful than this woman's actions. The woman's sin demanded that she be stoned. The religious crowd wanted Jesus to give an order for execution. Jesus told them that whoever was without sin could cast the first stone. They all left beginning with the eldest to the youngest as they were convicted by their own conscience. You see, we all have a stone to throw. We just do not have the right to throw it. Jesus was without sin. He could have stoned this woman and justly so. Jesus could have applied the letter of the law, but Jesus went beyond justice and spared the woman. Her accusers vanished when their own sin was brought to light. This woman appears to have a penitent heart toward her sin. Jesus did not stone her. He told her to go and sin no more. He went beyond justice to mercy. He went beyond the letter of the law with a gracious and forgiving spirit. He dealt with the woman's sin but with the right spirit. Each of us stands condemned to die and pay the wages of our sin. That is the letter of the law. Jesus went beyond the letter of the law and died for us by taking our place. That is the doctrine of the substitutionary atonement. Something better than justice was mercy. It is the only reason we have a hope of heaven. Moderation brings compassion to our convictions and tempers our life with balance. *Matthew 5:7 Blessed are the merciful: for they shall obtain mercy.* Let us be careful to remember that God only grants mercy to those who show mercy. Paul reminded these ladies, and us as well, that Christ is standing by. He is looking on at all we think, say or do. *Proverbs 5:21 For the ways of man [are] before the eyes of the LORD, and he pondereth all his goings. Proverbs 15:3 The eyes of the LORD [are] in every place, beholding the evil and the good. 1 Peter 3:12 For the eyes of the Lord [are] over the righteous, and his ears [are open] unto their prayers: but the face of the Lord [is] against them that do evil.*

In verse six Paul tells us to *be careful for nothing.* What does this mean? It does not mean that we throw all caution to the wind and run headlong "by faith" into destruction. It means we are not to be anxious or be given to worry. Let us quickly, but carefully, notice that this is a divine imperative. It is a command not a request. It is a sin for a Christian to live in fear and anxiety when we know the God who redeemed us knows the future and has prepared a safe landing in spite of some stormy waters.

Martha was "careful" about many things. *Luke 10:41 And Jesus answered and said unto her, Martha, Martha, thou art careful and troubled about many things...*Martha had a troubled spirit because she was careful (anxious) about many *things.* Martha created anxiety in her life by worrying about things that were beyond her control and power. Far too many people bring needless worry and anxiety upon themselves in the very same manner. The word anxiety comes from the same root word as anger and refers to the physical act of choking. Worry will choke peace and faith out of your life. We are not to worry about "nothing." Too many good folks add much stress to their lives by worrying about the "nothings" of life. They worry about what things might be, but almost never come to pass. It seems silly to worry about nothing. If it is nothing, there is no cause to worry. There is an old saying that says, "Today is the tomorrow I was worried about yesterday." Christians are not to worry about tomorrow. We cannot borrow tomorrow's grace today. *Matthew 6:34 Take therefore no thought for the morrow: for the morrow shall take thought for the things of itself. Sufficient unto the day is the evil thereof.* Of all people, Christians have the least to care about. All the promises, provision and protection of God belong to us. Our church often sings that wonderful hymn "I Don't Know About Tomorrow."

I don't know about tomorrow

I just live from day to day

I don't borrow from its sunshine

For its skies may turn to gray

I don't worry o'er the future

For I know what Jesus said

And today I'll walk beside Him

For He knows what lies ahead

Many things about tomorrow

I don't seem to understand

But I know Who holds tomorrow

And I know He holds my hand

Christians are not to worry. We are to pray. We are to ask God for our needs and trust that He will supply them. In this verse, prayer is the asking. Supplication is the answering. God knows our requests. He wants us to ask. If we ask, He will supply our needs according to His will and His riches in glory. A wealthy widow from Philadelphia once asked Dr. G. Campbell Morgan, "Dr. Morgan, do you really think we should pray about the little things in our lives?" I have always loved his answer. Dr. Morgan replied in his very British manner, "Madam, can you mention anything in your life that is too big for God?"

God answers every prayer. I did not say that God grants every request. I do say that God answers every prayer. All prayer is answered by God by yes, no or not now. No is an answer. It has been said that God has a lot of spoiled children. Every time He tells one "no," they cry that He does not answer prayers. *Psalms 84:11 For the LORD God is a sun and shield: the LORD will give grace and glory: no good thing will he withhold from them that walk uprightly.* God only withholds bad things. He never withholds good things. If God says no by withholding something from us, it means that it was not good for us, and we should be thankful that He did not allow something to come into our life that could cause us some future harm. He is protecting us. It has been said that when we pray we must remember three things- the love of God, the wisdom of God and the power of God. The love of God only wants what is best for us. The wisdom of God knows what is best for us. The power of God can give what is best for us.

The giving of thanks should accompany every prayer that is offered. When you have prayed, go ahead and thank God for His answer to your request. God wants us to come to Him in prayer and supplication without forgetting all the good He has already done for us. We are not to forget past mercies and provisions, while we are beseeching God for present mercies and provisions.

Worry is the interest we pay on the debt of unbelief with which we have mortgaged life. Faith ends where anxiety begins, so never give way to anxiety. ~Lehman Strauss

There is nothing too great for God's power; and nothing too small for His fatherly care. ~Unknown

A brave man never dies but once- a coward is dying all the time. ~Unknown

First, never fret or be anxious about a thing you can help. If you can help it, just help it and quit worrying. Second, never fret about a thing you can't help, for fretting won't do any good. ~ The father of B.H. Carroll

Our great matters are little to His power: our little matters are great to His love.

Be careful for nothing.

Be prayerful for everything.

Be thankful for anything.

Let your riches consist, not in the largeness of your possessions, but in the fewness of your wants. ~D.L. Moody

Gratitude to God for what He does give us will surely incline Him to grant what we do not have. ~Henry Halley

Do not reduce the Infinite to finite by placing a limit on Him. ~Lehman Strauss

And...here is a conjunction that connects answers to prayer. God yokes an answer of peace to prayer. God is the God of all peace. No one can grant us peace no matter how much they desire to do so. Neither can we create peace for ourselves, but we can receive an answer of peace in our prayers. Paul teaches us in verse seven that peace is the result of prayer, since prayer has the ability to bring peace. Someone once said that peace is the fruit that is born on the tree of prayer. When we have prayed, we can leave all things in the hands of the God of peace. Paul tells us that the peace of God passes all understanding. This does not mean that it is an unsolvable mystery. It means that although it is beyond our comprehension, we may give testimony to its full effect on our soul and our spirit. I cannot explain God's peace, but I have experienced it. Experience does not always require explanation. I do not have to worry about the criticisms and divisions of Euodias and Syntyche if I have the peace of God.

Remember that there is "peace with God" and the "peace of God." The first is my standing. The second is my state. I have peace with God through the blood of the cross. Peace *with* God is irrevocable. I cannot lose my standing (salvation) with God. I am eternally secure. The peace *of* God is my state according to my present earthly conditions. *John 14:27 Peace I leave with you, my peace I give unto you: not as the world giveth, give I unto you. Let not your heart be troubled, neither let it be afraid.* The world gives a false peace. They give a false feeling of security. The world finds peace in financial security, good health, or even personal philosophy. Their peace is temporary and easily lost. The peace that Jesus gives is tried and true. It is both pure and secure.

God can *keep* us in peace. The word that Paul uses here for *keep* is a military word for standing guard. The result of the prayer of faith is that God places His peace like a sentry standing guard over our hearts and minds. Jesus Christ stands guard at the door of the heart and mind of those who pray. He will protect them and keep them in peace. This is a divinely exceeding great and precious promise.

These Apostles of Christ, who breathed His peace, did not fear the unknown, since it was known to Him; did not fear the future, for it was present to Him; were not startled at the change in circumstances, since their peace did not depend on external things, but upon Him who is First and Last, and who guaranteed the supply of all need. ~F.B. Meyer

The human mind will always think on something. We must be very careful with our thoughts. *Proverbs 23:7 For as he thinketh in his heart, so is he: Eat and drink, saith he to thee; but his heart is not with thee.* Our thoughts determine our actions. They prepare us for action.

Our character takes on the complexion and hue of our inward thinking. ~F.B. Meyer

Satan has filled this world with every evil vice in an attempt to steal our thoughts. We have weak Christians because we have weak minds. We have allowed the filth of this world to enter our minds and empty us of God's power. In John Bunyan's *Pilgrim's Progress,* we find that Ignorance said: *"My heart is as good as many man's heart...As to my thoughts, I take no notice of them."* There are many people who never think about their thoughts.   F.B. Meyer said that they "...leave the castle gate of their soul perfectly open for any intruder that may wish to enter, either from heaven or hell; and so it befalls that the thoughts which are inspired by demons, but which are arrayed in the garb of respectable citizens, pour into the great gateway of the soul, filling the courtyard with their tumultuous uproar...If you could visit this world in the future, you would find that the falsehoods which now stalk across its arena, and seem as strong as thistles in spring, will have passed away." We must bring every thought into captivity to the obedience of Christ- 2 Corinthians 10:5. Verse eight is a filter for the filth of this world that the devil wants to infiltrate into our lives. Paul wanted the church at Philippi to set their minds on good things. These are the things that will strengthen our hearts and minds in Christ Jesus.

We also do not want to let our thoughts be consumed with things that will disappoint us or people (such as Euodias and Syntyche) who will break our hearts with their divisions. Someone once said that, "People come to church to eye the clothes or close the eyes." Euodias and Syntyche could think critically of each other, or they could remember that they are both redeemed children of God and sisters in Christ. This formula keeps us forbearing one another in love instead of scratching each other's eyes out.

Verse eight has been called the shortest biography of Christ. It is certainly a glimpse into the mind of Christ that is to be within every one of us. These thoughts are to govern our mind. There are seven qualities that are to be at the epicenter of all our thoughts:

- ✟ Honest
- ✟ Just
- ✟ Pure
- ✟ Lovely
- ✟ Good Report
- ✟ Virtue
- ✟ Praise

Our first thoughts must be *honest*. This is a word that was used by the Greeks to speak of gods and the temple of the gods. The idea that Paul is trying to convey to the church is to think as one who moves through life as if the whole world is the temple of God. This is the person who keeps God in all his thoughts. *1 Chronicles 28:9 And thou, Solomon my son, know thou the God of thy father, and serve him with a perfect heart and with a willing mind: for the LORD searcheth all hearts, and understandeth all the imaginations of the thoughts: if thou seek him, he will be found of thee; but if thou forsake him, he will cast thee off for ever. Psalms 10:4 The wicked, through the pride of his countenance, will not seek [after God]: God [is] not in all his thoughts.* One who is honest will take life seriously. They will see the hand of

216

God in all things. They will be continuously conscious of the presence of God in every moment of their life. Again, Charles Spurgeon said that there was never more than a quarter of an hour that passed in his life that he was not aware of the presence of God in his life. Those who keep God in all their thoughts will walk honestly towards all men.

Our second thought must be *just*. To think on things that are just means that we are constantly mindful of our duties to God and to our fellow man. *Micah 6:8 He hath shewed thee, O man, what is good; and what doth the LORD require of thee, but to do justly, and to love mercy, and to walk humbly with thy God?* A Christian must maintain a constant vigil in the mind to fulfill God's requirement to be just in all we do. We are admonished to consider how we treat people. We are to treat people right.

Our next thought must be *pure*. There are things that might be both honest and just, but they might not be pure. The honest truth might reveal some sin. Justice must bring judgment upon sin. So there is a need for our thoughts to be pure. The word pure, as it is used here, describes that which has been cleansed so that it is fit to be brought into the presence of God. *Psalms 24:3-4 Who shall ascend into the hill of the LORD? or who shall stand in his holy place? He that hath clean hands, and a pure heart; who hath not lifted up his soul unto vanity, nor sworn deceitfully.* Christians are to be mindful to keep themselves pure so that they are always prepared to be in the presence of God. The right motive will keep a pure heart. The proper motivation is to please God and walk in fellowship and obedience to Him. How many times have we gone to pray with some unconfessed sin in our life? The Bible teaches us that to come to God in this manner is pride in our own power. God has said that He will break the pride of our power and make our heaven as iron and our earth as brass when it comes to our prayers. Our prayers will not get past the ceiling if we cannot present ourselves to God as a pure and a living sacrifice. God examines the thoughts of every man. He knows whether or not we are pure in our heart and mind. *Psalms 139:23 Search me, O God, and know my heart: try me, and know my thoughts...*

Our next admonition is to think on things that are *lovely*. This command has in it the idea to think on those things that bring forth love. There are many who set their minds to vengeance, bitterness, criticism and rebuke. Their thoughts are full of resentment, and they cause others to resent them in turn. As a child of God we should set our mind to love all men and to bring out the best in people.

Paul's next exhortation is to think on things of *good report*. This word means "well spoken" or "reputable." I was taught long ago to "consider the source" whenever I heard any report whether good or bad. Not everyone is a good source for good news. It is a shame that bad news travels quickest, and many good reports will not be issued until God reads them from the Book of Works at the Judgment Seat of Christ. A good report also conveys the idea of "speaking things which are fit for God to hear." Many Christians would have little or nothing to say if they simply followed this simple piece of advice. I have a friend who I know is very well informed. By that I mean that people love to call him with the latest garbage that is going around. Many times through the years I have heard some bad news (bad report) and later it was revealed that he was aware of it prior to my hearing of it. He never wants to be the one that gives the bad news. He has a good reputation because he gives good reports. Bad news does travel fast, but it does not have to travel through us. Let us speak only the things which are fit for God to hear.

Our next thought is to be one of *virtue*. This is not a word that is common to our vocabulary these days, but it should be. If it were part of our thought life, it would become more common. This is the only time that Paul uses this particular word for virtue in any of his writings. It is the Greek word *arête*. It means "excellence." It describes every kind of excellence. We are to think of things that excel. My father's preacher, Pastor William B. Mussellman, used to always say, "Accentuate the positive. Don't dwell on the negative." There are low thoughts that will drag you down to fear, despair and doubt. There are high thoughts that will strengthen your heart and mind and take you closer to God.

Finally, we come to *praise*. Never a thought should enter the mind of a Christian that cannot end with praise to God. If you cannot praise God for it, it should be banished from your mind. We must be mindful to be quick to praise and slow to critique. How much happier and pleasant life at Philippi will be if the church is filled with thoughts of praise that flow from the lips of God's people. Let there always be a word of praise in our mouth. Find something good to say about someone or something. When you can think of nothing or no one to praise, there is always something to praise God about. As the Doxology teaches us, let us continually praise God from Whom all blessings flow. *Psalms 150:6 Let every thing that hath breath praise the LORD. Praise ye the LORD.*

Paul tells us to *think on these things.* It has been well said that you cannot prevent a bird from flying over your head, but you can prevent it from building a nest in your hair. Let these thoughts be the keepers of the gate of your soul. Let them be sentries that admit only those thoughts that may enter under the banner of these qualities.

In verse nine we learn that Christians are not just to meditate on certain things. There are certain things we are to do. These meditations would transform their activities. The Philippians had both learned and received certain things from Paul. They learned and then they received by accepting the things they had learned into practical application in life. Many hear and never learn. Many also learn but never *receive* or take the things they have learned to heart to be put to good use. *John 13:17 If ye know these things, happy are ye if ye do them.*

Personal example is an essential part of teaching. A good teacher will always demonstrate by their actions the truths which they are seeking to convey to their students. A good woodshop teacher will not just tell the students how to run a machine. He will demonstrate it. We learn through both the ear gate and the eye gate. Someone is watching what we do and hearing what we say. It is going to make an impression on their character. We must "practice what we preach." Paul was a good example to follow. Jeremiah said that he would get himself to the great men for they had known the way of the Lord. Thank the Lord for good examples. We need to strive to follow good examples and set a good example. Someone is always coming behind us. It is always easiest to walk in the path well-trodden. I have walked on paths in Africa as old as the time of Abraham. Man and beast have followed the same well-worn path for centuries simply because someone had already walked there. They build their new roads next to the old paths because everyone knows the well-worn paths that are thousands of years old. Leave a good path to follow. *Hebrews 13:7 Remember them which have the rule over you, who have spoken unto you the word of God: whose faith follow, considering the end of their conversation.* Follow those leaders of faith in your life considering the end of their life and the eternal rewards that await them so that you might reap the same.

In verse seven we have the peace of God. In verse nine we have the God of peace. The *God of peace* is Paul's favorite title for God in his epistles. He uses it more than a dozen times. Peace is not simply the absence of trouble. It is even more so the blessed assurance of the heart. The God of peace keeps us out of the pit of despair. Peace is not subdued. It is victorious.

We have the sweet assurance that "the God of peace shall be with you" thus connecting all this with the promise of verse seven above, where we are assured that the "peace of God" shall garrison the minds and hearts of all who cast their every care on Him. ~Dr. Henry Ironside

Philippi's Provision- Philippians 4:10-23

Philippians 4:10-23 *But I rejoiced in the Lord greatly, that now at the last your care of me hath flourished again; wherein ye were also careful, but ye lacked opportunity. Not that I speak in respect of want: for I have learned, in whatsoever state I am, therewith to be content. I know both how to be abased, and I know how to abound: every where and in all things I am instructed both to be full and to be hungry, both to abound and to suffer need. I can do all things through Christ which strengtheneth me. Notwithstanding ye have well done, that ye did communicate with my affliction. Now ye Philippians know also, that in the beginning of the gospel, when I departed from Macedonia, no church communicated with me as concerning giving and receiving, but ye only. For even in Thessalonica ye sent once and again unto my necessity. Not because I desire a gift: but I desire fruit that may abound to your account. But I have all, and abound: I am full, having received of Epaphroditus the things which were sent from you, an odour of a sweet smell, a sacrifice acceptable, wellpleasing to God. But my God shall supply all your need according to his riches in glory by Christ Jesus. Now unto God and our Father be glory for ever and ever. Amen. Salute* *every saint in Christ Jesus. The brethren which are with me greet you. All the saints salute you, chiefly they that are of Caesar's household. The grace of our Lord Jesus Christ be with you all. Amen.*

In verses eleven through thirteen there are seven great lessons for Christians to learn:

1. How to be content in all circumstances.
2. How to be abased in all things and all places.
3. How to abound in all things and all places.
4. How to be full.
5. How to be hungry.
6. How to suffer need.
7. How all things are possible through Christ.

Once again, Paul has a great reason to rejoice in verse ten. In verse four Paul told Philippi to rejoice in the Lord. We see here that Paul himself was rejoicing greatly in the Lord. He was a good example. Paul was not asking them to do something he was not doing himself. Paul rejoiced in dire circumstances. He was imprisoned with an unknown future, yet he rejoiced greatly for the greatness and the power of the God he served and loved was undiminished. God is just as great whether we are bound in prison or seated on a throne in a palace.

Remember there was a period of about two years (after he had been in Jerusalem) that the church at Philippi had lost contact with him. Once they made contact with him again at Rome, they began to care for him again. Paul had not been in Philippi for ten to twelve years, yet they immediately began to meet his needs as they had before. Christian contact equals compassionate care.

Paul was not sitting discontentedly in prison in Rome. He was not pouting. It is said that John Wesley once remarked that he did not know which dishonored God the most-to worry which is to doubt God's love and care or to curse and swear. Paul had long ago learned how to be content no matter what his circumstances might be. This is a great lesson for every child of God. I often say that happiness is determined by what is "happening" in your life. Joy is determined by your relationship with Jesus. When you have a good relationship with Jesus, you are not tossed to and fro by the ever changing circumstances of life. You live by contentment.

Paul used the Greek word *autarkes*. *Autarkes* is a word of both Greek and Roman ethics that means "entirely self-sufficient." It was the highest aim of the Stoics who came along in the third century. The Stoics were a group of philosophers from Athens who tried to eliminate emotions and desire. They believed that a man was made happy, not by adding to his possessions, but by taking away his wealth. They believed in eliminating all emotion until you did not care what happened to yourself. They tried to abolish the feelings of the heart. Someone once said that the Stoics made the heart a desert and called it peace. For the Stoics contentment was a human achievement. For Paul it was a gift of God that never killed the affections of the heart.

Contentment is not based on possessions but on our position in Christ. Contentment has the same relationship with Christ whether you are in the day of plenty or poverty. I know a man who I used to attend church with in Iowa. He owns a small body shop. He is a very happy Christian and always takes good care of people. There is a sign on the outside of his shop right next to the door as you would go into his office. It says, "Happiness isn't having what you want. It's wanting what you have." I thought that was a great testimony and later learned it meant even more coming from this man. His father had an invention and owned exclusive rights to it. The father became ill with cancer. He was going to die soon. He did not want his family to be burdened with debts. He sold the rights to his invention, thinking the money would pay for the hospital bills when he died. As it turned out, the man fully recovered from the cancer. He sold his invention, and others made a fortune from it. I never knew the father, but I am told though he was certainly disappointed, he was never bitter. Neither was the son who surely would have inherited a fortune. Their family was living by contentment. It too often seems that the more we have, the more discontented we are and the more we are prone to complain. Contentment has often been found missing in the homes of the rich only to be discovered in the homes of the poor. *Luke 12:15 And he said unto them, Take heed, and beware of covetousness: for a man's life consisteth not in the abundance of the things which he possesseth.* Contentment is a lesson to be learned. It is a difficult lesson to learn early in our Christian life. Those who will devote themselves to learning this lesson will live with an abundance of grace and a fullness of peace, joy and love.

We become rich either by possessing the abundance of this world, or by losing our desire for it, by abounding in everything, or by being content to have nothing; and surely the two conditions in such a changeful world as this, the latter is both safer and happier. To have little and to be content with it, is better than to have great riches invested in the Stock Exchange, where a man may be a millionaire today and a pauper tomorrow. ~F.B. Meyer

It is difficult to walk in the clear day of prosperity without wandering, or in the dark day of adversity without stumbling. ~D.L Moody

Paul tells us in verse twelve that he was the same Christian in times of plenty and times of leanness. He knew how to be thankful when he was full and how to be just as thankful when he was hungry. When his life abounded with blessings, he never forgot where they came from. He was thankful and rejoiced that God had given him all things richly to enjoy. When he suffered a need, he simply saw an opportunity for God to take care of him and to provide his lack of supply from the storehouse of heaven.

Many expect God's servants to abase themselves. Very few rejoice when God makes His servants to abound. There will be lean years and good years in the life of a Christian just as there were in the land of

Egypt. Often the servant who has been abased for a long period of time feels guilty when God gives an abundance. Dr. Ironside used to tell the story of how he used to preach at Mel Trotter's mission in Grand Rapids, Michigan on a yearly basis. Mel Trotter has been called the worst drunk to ever get saved. He devoted his life to winning drunks to the Lord. He led a drunk to the Lord whose life was gloriously changed. The man opened a brand new hotel in Grand Rapids, Michigan. That hotel owner told Mel Trotter, "When you have a speaker or visitor come to your mission, you send him over to the hotel. We will keep him here free of charge." When Dr. Ironside came, they put him in the presidential suite. Dr. Ironside had never stayed any place as nice as this suite. It bothered him. He called Mel Trotter up on the phone and said, "Mel, you don't have to put me up like this. I don't need all this luxury. All I want is a room with a comfortable bed, and a desk and a lamp where I can study." Mel assured him that the room was not costing him or the mission anything. It was being provided at no cost. Mel Trotter said to Dr. Ironside, "Harry, Paul said he knew how to abound and he knew how to be abased. Now you learn to abound this week, will you?"

Many Christians claim verse thirteen as their life verse. It is a an exceeding great and precious promise, as Peter would say, and this is no idle boast from Paul. This is the declaration of a godly man testifying to the power of the indwelling Christ. Paul lived independent of circumstance and yet totally dependent on Christ.

God always empowers us to do all things whatsoever He has commanded us- Matthew 28:19-20. Whatever God has for you to do for Him, He always gives you the power to do it. God gives every Christian a spiritual gift. He also gives the power and the wisdom to exercise it. When God calls, God qualifies. *All things* does not mean all the things we desire. God would never put unlimited power in the hands of His people so they could do whatever they wanted. Eventually, our flesh would make merchandise of the power of God and do great damage. God never empowers the flesh to do the works of the flesh. *All things* is the things that God has for us according to His will.

Another mistake that causes many Christians to fail in the work of God is that they labor in the power of the flesh and not the Spirit. J. Vernon McGhee used to liken this verse to a train running on its tracks. He used to describe a train called the Super Chief that ran from Los Angeles to Chicago. The train had the ability to travel with tremendous power over the tracks, even up the Cajon Pass, the highest pass in America any train must travel over; however, the train must stay on the tracks. If the engineer decided he would like to turn off and see the Grand Canyon, the train would derail and be a wreck. There are no tracks to take them there. The minute a child of God leaves the will of God, their life immediately becomes worse than a train wreck. This verse does not teach that the Christian does everything for himself. Nor does it teach that God does everything for the Christian. It does not teach us that Christ does everything while we do nothing. It does teach us that God will empower us to do the things He has called us to do. God is liable when we are responsible. We can rely on God. Can God rely on us to do His will? Paul continued faithfully in *all things* for many years. God strengthened Paul to do His will and get through- 2 Corinthians 12. Paul was continually in peril, labors abundant, stripes above measure, prisons frequent, faced death often, fought with the beasts of Ephesus, thrice beaten with rods, stoned, shipwrecked, robbed, hungry and cold. God's grace and strength was sufficient to get him through his troubles. God does not strengthen us for all the things we would like to do, but He does for all the things He has called us to do. *Isaiah 40:29 He giveth power to the faint; and to them that have no might he increaseth strength.* God's ability to supply is far greater than our needs. *Jeremiah 33:3 Call unto me, and I will answer thee, and shew thee great and mighty things, which thou knowest not.* God will be a debtor to no man.

In verses fourteen through nineteen Paul references the care that Philippi had bestowed upon him on more than one occasion. In Acts 16-17 we learned how Paul planted the church in Philippi. He then moved on to Thessalonica and Berea. As he traveled across Macedonia and eventually on to Athens and Corinth, only Philippi showed the proof of their love by supporting Paul financially in the work of the Gospel. Philippi was the first church to support a missionary. What a high and noble honor! When Paul labored in Corinth, the church there did nothing for Paul as he labored among them. He told them that he robbed churches of wages that he might labor among them (2

Corinthians 11:7-12), and he worked willingly with his own hands as a tent maker with Priscilla and Aquila (Acts 18). Only Philippi ministered to him when he was afflicted. The word affliction here does not mean a physical affliction but an affliction of tribulation. He had financial needs, and God used the church at Philippi to meet them. The word communicate means to share. They shared in Paul's labors in the gospel by supporting him financially. Every soul that was saved was fruit that was credited to their account in heaven as well. Paul and Philippi shared the fruit of the gospel. Paul labored and they gave. Everyone is either called to send or be sent. Remember that an apostle is a "sent one." Philippi's job was to send so they could share in the work of the gospel. In Thessalonica Paul both worked and was supported by the church at Philippi. The same was true of Corinth. Paul planted churches in countless cities in Europe and Asia, and only the church at Philippi supported him along the way. This small church lying in an obscure place at the outskirts of the Roman Empire was diligent to keep track of Paul as best they could and send to his needs once and again.

Paul was eternally grateful for their gift. It was sorely needed, but not asked for. He did not even desire their gift, but God always blesses His people through His people and the church at Philippi had caught this valuable lesson. He knew God would take care of him as He always had. The Lord took care of him during the two years Philippi lost track of him. His great joy was not that his need had been met, but he rejoiced that the Philippians would be partakers of his reward. He wanted them to share in the reward more than he desired his personal needs to be met. Giving is a continual and essential part of the Christian life. God rewards the tangible with the eternal. Some will abound in grace and eternal rewards while others will see less of God's grace on earth and little of God's rewards in heaven.

Any gift, whether to the Lord's work or the Lord's workmen, is of greater worth and high significance when viewed as a gift to God. ~Dr. Lehman Strauss

The lesson holds for us, in our missionary offerings, of the modern world. Each offering, just a mite of an offering, does not amount to much. But even as the tiny raindrops that fall all over Niagara Falls, so these mites of offerings from hundreds of thousands of Christians all over the land together constitute the stream of funds which is supporting the vast army of foreign missionaries out on the far-flung battle lines of the Cross, enduring hardships we would not think of enduring here at home, the noblest army of men and women the sun ever shone on. Those who, by their offerings to Missions, make themselves a part of this mightiest movement of all the ages, will, in the day of final reckoning, be entitled to share in its rewards. ~Henry Halley

Everyone has an account in heaven. The word account is found six times in the New Testament in reference to our account that is in heaven. These Scriptures teach us what we will give an account for on the Day of Judgment.   These are the things that God holds us responsible for on earth:

1. Every idle word- Matthew 12:36
2. Our service- Matthew 18:23; 1 Corinthians 4:1
3. Our stewardship- Luke 16:2
4. Our testimony before other believers and the lost- Romans 14:12
5. Our giving- Philippians 4:17
6. Our obedience to those who are in authority over us- Hebrews 13:17

Epaphroditus was the one who brought this love offering to Paul from the church at Philippi. Paul rejoiced when he saw Epaphroditus. His rejoicing increased as he saw the gifts they had sent him. This church brought joy to one who was suffering on behalf of Christ. When a Christian gives, it is like a priest making an offering to God. When a child of God gives from the heart with the right spirit, God sees our tangible offering on earth as a spiritual sacrifice in heaven.

In Leviticus 1:9 we are told that the burnt offerings that ascended from the altar were *a sweet savour unto the Lord.* In Ephesians Paul used this same word when speaking of the Lord. *Ephesians 5:2 And walk in love, as Christ also hath loved us, and hath given himself for us an offering and a sacrifice to God for a sweetsmelling savour.* The death of Jesus was costly and therefore worth much to God. When a child of God makes a sacrificial offering, no matter how little or how much, God accepts it and His pleasure is measured according to the love from our heart with which it is offered. Real Christianity does not give from compulsion or law but is constrained by love. *2 Corinthians 9:6-9 But this I say, He which soweth sparingly shall reap also sparingly; and he which soweth bountifully shall reap also bountifully. Every man according as he purposeth in his heart, so let him give; not grudgingly, or of necessity: for God loveth a cheerful giver. And God is able to make all grace abound toward you; that ye, always having all sufficiency in all things, may abound to every good work: (As it is written, He hath dispersed abroad; he hath given to the poor: his righteousness remaineth for ever.* Christ did not give grudgingly or sparingly. Christ gave Himself both willingly and fully from the depths of His love. Those offerings given grudgingly and sparingly do not ascend as a sweet savour to God, and they will not reap the abundance of God's graces. God wants our giving to come from willing and loving hearts motivated by devotion to God.

Paul received the gift not because he desired to profit by means of their generosity, but because he saw in it an added evidence of the working of the Spirit of grace in their souls, and this was for their blessing, as well as relieving his need. And so he gladly accepted it all, seeing in it "an odor of a sweet savor, a sacrifice acceptable and well-pleasing to God." ~Dr. Henry Ironside

Verse nineteen is both a powerful and a present promise today. Paul thought of the sacrifice they had made to meet his personal needs. He knew they had needs of their own. I do not know anyone who does not have needs. We are a needy people living in a needy world. We have needs from the moment we draw our first breath until we have breathed our last. The Philippians put Paul's needs above their own personal needs. God promised they would not suffer for it. I have never seen anyone go broke giving to the work of God. I have never seen anyone any poorer for a gift given to God. The wealth of God is open to those who prove their love towards all men by supporting the work of the missionary. You can be broke on earth and have millions in heaven. We must be careful to remember that this verse is not given as a blanket promise to all Christians. It is only for those who will support the work of the gospel. Only those who give to missions can claim the power and promise of this verse. It is a conditional promise, but it is a certain provision for those who will be obedient to it.

We must remember who is supplying our needs- God. Paul said, *my God.* God owns the earth and the fulness thereof. He inhabits the heavens and the heaven of heavens. He owns every beast of the forest and the cattle on a thousand hills- Psalms 50:10. He has the ability and the resources to meet our needs. There is a rich source of supply. This is not a vain promise.

We must also understand the sufficiency of this promise. God promises to meet our need not our greed. A desire is not a need. A need is something necessary to sustain our life. Our needs are large to us but little to God. There is nothing so great that Go is not able to supply. It is sad that often needs that could be met are not. I believe that Jesus taught us this in the Sermon on the Mount. I believe that the epicenter of the Sermon on the Mount is a foreshadow given to the church concerning missions giving. We always preach about our faith promise that we make to God in a missions conference. In Matthew 6:19-33 God makes a faith promise to us. There was once an old and poverty-stricken Indian who lived in the days following the American Revolution. He made his way to a western settlement in search of food to keep from starving. He had a brightly colored ribbon around his neck. A small dirty pouch hung from the ribbon. Someone asked him what was in the pouch. He said it was a charm given to him in his younger days. He opened it and pulled out a very old crumpled piece of paper. It was a discharge from the continental army personally signed by General George Washington. It entitled him to a life-long pension for his service in the Army. This man had a signed promissory note that entitled him to never go hungry, but he never claimed the promise. It is sad that many Christians have a more faithful promise that they allow to go unclaimed.

So many look at this verse as simply a financial promise. They are short changing themselves. We have many more needs than just financial needs. The Bible promises "all" of our needs. This includes our emotional, physical, spiritual, social and financial needs. This is a New Testament promise that was given in Psalm 23 of the Old Testament. If God's promises fail, nothing is certain, and faith is futile. We would do well to examine how the Bible defines riches:

- ✤ The riches of God's goodness- Romans 2:4.
- ✤ The riches of God's wisdom- Romans 11:33.
- ✤ The riches of God's grace- Ephesians 1:7.
- ✤ The riches of God's glory- Ephesians 3:16.

Not that giving to the Lord should be looked upon as a reciprocal trade agreement. We should not give to get; but our giving to the Lord will always insure our getting from the Lord. Nothing that we give to the Lord is overlooked. On the other hand, what grounds have we to lay hold of this promise to supply our needs if we have refused to supply the needs of God's work when we had the means? With what confidence can we pray for the Lord to honour us with substance if we have not honoured Him with the substance that He has already given? This is an ageless principle in the economy of God: what we withhold, withers, but what we scatter, gathers; what we lay aside, spoils, but what we release, returns. If we will "fill full" another's needs, God will "full fill" our needs. ~J. H. Pickford

Paul begins to close out this epistle in verse twenty. In closing, Paul once again glorifies God. It should be the continual practice, and growing habit of the child of God, to give thanks and praise to God for all He has done for us. Christians should be ever mindful to give glory to God as grateful creatures of a wise and kind Creator. More than that, our Creator is our eternal everlasting Father. It is the nature of fathers to look out for the needs of their children. Our Father in heaven is attentive to our needs. May we be quick to offer Him the little He requires- a heart that is eternally filled with thanks and praise.

After Paul gives God the glory, he then greets the saints. The Christians in Rome had never met the saints in Philippi, yet there was a kindred Spirit that bound them together. Their love for Christ was a sweet tie that wished them to be remembered by Paul. Many of the names of Roman Christians mentioned in Romans 16 are identical to those names inscribed on sepulchers belonging to the imperial household.

The phrase *Caesar's household* was a broad term for all those who labored in what we might call the imperial civil service. Caesar's household had members all over the Roman empire. Paul's labors had infiltrated the highest citizens of the empire. Paul won many government officials to Christ and saw them added to the church.

It is as possible to be a Christian in a royal court as in a slum. ~F.B. Meyer

Here is one final reason to rejoice. Grace has the last word. We may always rejoice in the presence of our Lord and Savior Jesus Christ as He fills our lives with His abundant grace. When life is over and it is all said and done, the last word will be one of God's grace to His people. *Revelation 22:21 The grace of our Lord Jesus Christ be with you all. Amen.*

Bibliography

Barclay, William *The Letters To the Philippians.* Louisville, Kentucky; Westminster John Knox Press; copyright 2003

Carroll, B.H. *An Interpretation of the English Bible.* Grand Rapids, Michigan; Baker Book House; copyright 1948, Broadman Press

Halley, Henry. *Halley's Bible Handbook.* Grand Rapids, Michigan; Zondervan Publishing House; copyright 1927

Henry, Matthew. *Matthew Henry's Commentary on the Whole Bible.* Peabody, Massachusetts; Hendrickson Publishers Marketing, LLC; copyright 1991

Ironside, Henry. *Philippians.* Neptune, New Jersey; Loizeaux Brothers, Inc.; copyright 1947

Meyer, F.B. *Devotional Commentary on Philippians.* Grand Rapids, Michigan; Kregel Publications; copyright 1979

Moody, D.L. *Moody's Notes from My Bible and Anecdotes & Illustrations.* St. John, Indiana. The Christian Book Gallery; copyright 1895

Strauss, Lehman. *Philippians.* Neptune, New Jersey; Loizeaux Brothers, Inc.; copyright 1959

www.ingramcontent.com/pod-product-compliance
Lightning Source LLC
Chambersburg PA
CBHW051819090426

42736CB00011B/1562